DIAGRAM.2

THE SECOND PRINT ANTHOLOGY
FEATURING SELECTIONS
FROM YEARS 3-4 OF THE
EXCELLENT ONLINE MAGAZINE
OF TEXT, ART & SCHEMATIC
WHICH IS MOSTLY AVAILABLE AT:

HTTP://THEDIAGRAM.COM

DIAGRAM.2

The Second Print Anthology Featuring Selections from Years 3-4 of the Excellent Online Magazine of Text, Art & Schematic which is Mostly Available at:

http://thediagram.com

Edited by Ander Monson

— Del Sol Press ♦ Washington, D.C. —

DIAGRAM.2: The Second Print Anthology

Ander Monson, Editor. Copyright © 2006 by DIAGRAM. All Rights Reserved.

DEL SOL PRESS, WASHINGTON, D.C.
PAPER ISBN: 0-9762092-1-7.

First Edition.

Cover and Interior Design by Ander Monson.

Much of the material contained herein originally appeared in DIAGRAM, a magazine of text, art, and schematic, which can be found online at <THEDIAGRAM.COM>, mirrored at Web del Sol, <WEBDELSOL.COM>.

Source materials for images are noted in the acknowledgments page towards the end of the book. The cover image is taken from a July 1905 ad from *American Homes and Gardens* magazine for the "A. C. / Anti-Cancer) Pipe."

We have made our best attempts to obtain permission to reprint the images herein; if you are the copyright holder of an image and object to its reproduction in these pages, please contact us.

This book was produced in cooperation with DIAGRAM and the New Michigan Press.

HTTP://THEDIAGRAM.COM
HTTP://NEWMICHIGANPRESS.COM

EDITOR@THEDIAGRAM.COM / NMP@THEDIAGRAM.COM

CONTENTS

Nin Andrews	3		87	Austin Hummell
Christopher Arigo	4		91	Melanie Jordan
R. S. Armstrong	6		101	Melanie Kenny
Amanda Auchter	9		102	C. F. Kimball
JoAnn Balingit	10		105	Matthew Kirby
Michele Battiste	12		109	L. S. Klatt
Robin Behn	16		111	Sharon Kraus
F. J. Bergmann	18		112	Corinne Lee
Joe Bisz	21		113	Matthew Lippman
Sarah Blackman	23		115	Duane Locke
Anne Boyer	25		118	Daniel Mahoney
Jason Bredle	28		121	Barbara Maloutas
Carrie Comer	34		122	Peter Markus
Greg Darms	37		125	Clay Matthews
Barbara DeCesare	39		127	Deirdra McAfee
Spencer Dew	41		137	Jeffrey Morgan
Tim Earley	46		138	Rachel Moritz
Jim Fisher	54		146	Simone Muench
Angela Jane Fountas	55		148	Mark Neely
Jamey Gallagher	60		150	Lindsay Packer
Alice George	61		152	Pedro Ponce
Jonathan Gibbs	67		153	Joshua Poteat
Don Gilliland	71		156	Billy Reynolds
Susan Goslee	72		160	Mary Ann Rockwell
Andrew C. Gottlieb	74		161	Michael J. Rosen
Rae Gouirand	75		165	F. Daniel Rzicznek
Arielle Greenberg	77		168	Zachary Schomburg
Kate Greenstreet	79		170	Eric Schwerer
Molly Bianca Gross	80		171	Alan Semerdjian
Matthew Guenette	81		177	Ron Singer
Paul Guest	83		187	Marcus Slease
Annalynn Hammond	85		188	Bruce Smith

CONTENTS (CONTINUED)

Sara Jane Stoner	192
Jay Surdukowski	202
Molly Tenenbaum	206
John Terry	212
Jen Tynes	218
Jane Unrue	222
Gautam Verma	226
Virgil (Trans. Kimberly Johnson)	228
Benjamin Vogt	230
G. C. Waldrep	232
Fritz Ward	235
Joshua Marie Wilkinson	240
Susan Settlemyre Williams	242
Steven Wingate	246
Mark Yakich	248
Jake Adam York	250
Scott Zieher	252
Acknowledgments	255

A Note on this Artifact You Are Holding

THIS, OUR SECOND PRINT ANTHOLOGY, was produced with a significant amount of labor, especially from Tom Fleischmann, our Assistant Poetry Editor, who helped greatly with its research, selection, compilation, and editing.

SELECTIONS FOR THIS ANTHOLOGY were made from the work we've published online from issues 3.1 to 4.6. Our editors chose work specifically that translated well to the printed page, that we particularly loved. I wish we could have included everything we published online in these twelve issues, but then this book in your hands would be officially a Big-Assed Tome.

THANKS MUCH TO MY OTHER PARTNERS IN CRIME, particularly Poetry Editor Heidi Gotz, who has been here from the magazine's inception, and our Fiction Editor, Lauren Goodwin. Additional thanks go to Assistant / Contributing Editors Emma Ramey and Christopher Roman, and our newest additions to the force: Reviews Editor Megan Campbell, Assistant Fiction Editor Brian Buckbee, and Sonics Editor Shannon Fields.

—*Ander Monson, Editor*

(January 2006)

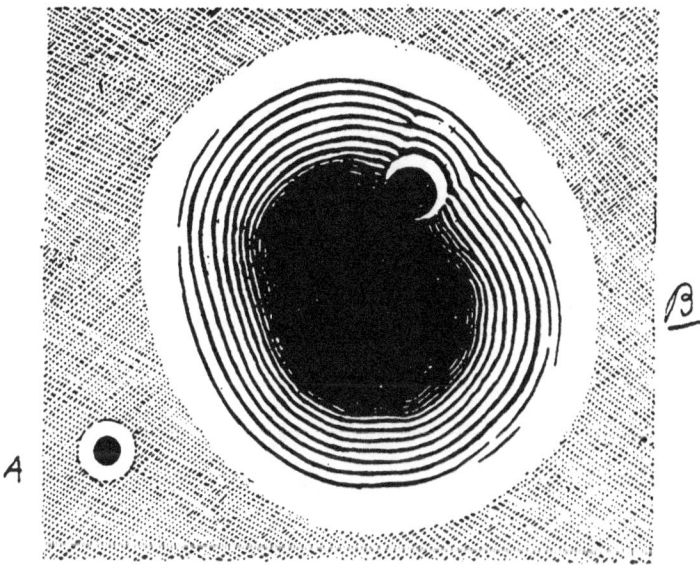

The smaller figure (*A*) shows the sphere of influence of the silver nitrate. The larger figure (*B*) shows the effect of the smaller when included in the larger. Note that the smaller sphere has removed the chromate so that the rings in the larger are interrupted.

Nin Andrews : BURNING POINT

Sometimes Greta knew the world was perfect, as perfect a Mozart concerto, and she wanted to feel it that way forever, like a tune inside her, or like a warm haze she sometimes felt when her mother stroked her back with Witch Hazel. But something always happened. Her mother crying, her father, leaving, her body falling. It reminded her of the day she watched Terrence Uchino playing with a magnifying glass, holding it over a dry leaf. At first it was nothing, then there was flame, tiny and yellow, eating the fringe, following its edges until it curled inwards towards the center in a gesture of helplessness. But what bothered Greta wasn't the end, the moment of blackening, of giving into the flame. It was that instant between flame and no flame. That split second when she held her breath, and then watched the first burst of fire, leaping, dancing, burning. How could she predict it? That moment. When everything changed.

Christopher Arigo : ABBREVIATED INDEX FOR NUCLEAR & PARTICLE PHYSICS

Accelerator You cannot see how your gaze upsets the seen—
indecisive: between place or time, between cat alive or cat dead.
Your manifesto of smashing for novelty, assembling refuse
into refusals with the sound of a television switched
off and fading. Your legs spark under sheets. **Backscatter**
When snapping dust reflects toward us, an excited
brume of **Decay** When phrases settle into matrices mapped
with red arrows and Xs or an unforeseen breakdown: enucleate
into nucleus, atomize into ato—verb to noun to verb—
into **Excited** particles When they assemble into a you, into
a we, forgotten or ignored in higher states of swirling energy
expressed—by you—by smashing windows and raising
your arms to welcome the diffracting splinters back to earth
or dancing in their **Scintillation** When air is charged by your static
and scent—of lilies and musk—then our hands blur
when moving, trailed by afterimages of hands after images
catch up to themselves, when **Strangeness Numbers** Or any
number of particles survive our proximity of one

Christopher Arigo : ABBREVIATED INDEX FOR OPTICS

Albedo See the ratio of how brilliantly you burn : the conflagration scintillating in your eyes : what remains unabsorbed : how your body reflects red near a brick building. **Coherent light** See how singularly you desire some system to circumscribe desire—beginning w/ what you believe you see, some somatic delusion. **Critical angle** See when your body is synonymous w/ incandescence. **Diffraction** See how your body emanates in infinite directions the tension between desire & necessity, the moment just after sleep & just before waking— how lucid dreams reflect you, the dreamer. **Focal point** See the convergence, real or apparent, of rays reflected by mirror. This is your visual echo. This is your **Illuminated body** See how you alter minute by minute as sun passes from zenith to nadir, how attuned your eyes are to any azimuth, the ratio of celestial body : celestial body. See angle, critical & the intensity of your flux, how you shimmer, how you collapse towards your vertex, how you implode w/ desire & radiant colors. Light means vision means mirror means to see

R. S. Armstrong : UNDERSTANDING FRACTIONS

1. Uses of Fractions

to make one wonder
to distance one's self
to wish for
to want (expression of)
to represent limitation
to close off an exit
to empty part-way
to leave ajar

2. Language of Fractions

half/whole
if any/few
(distractions, for instance)
absent/in the same room as
touching lightly/pressed together

3. Subtraction, Multiplication, Division

the room loses an entrance

the body loses a hand

the person enters, leaving the door ajar

4. Different Names for the Same Fractional Number

a wish granted but only partially
(a wish made and partially granted)

"Don't leave now, it's only __ o'clock"
"I must leave, it's already __ o'clock"
a trick of memory
a way to avoid disaster/embarrassment
abandonment/regret

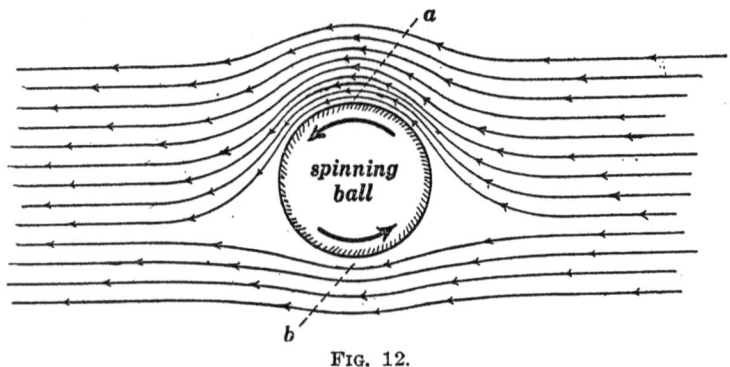

Fig. 12.

Amanda Auchter : WATER JEALOUSY

The sink fills with its tenants:
each side is a little apartment.

The fork tumbles first, its tines
a lost instrument. I carry its tune.

I could be rubber, I could be stone.

I resume my jealousy of solid objects,
fill all spaces: machine life, street life, sky life.

This is a world of floating continents—
last night's meal, the good china, body of glass.

An odd stick-woman shoos me away with a sponge.

Little green floatation device.

I feel a plate, I feel a drain.

JoAnn Balingit : YOUR HEART AND HOW IT WORKS

Your heart is a pump not much bigger than a sweet potato.
It weighs about half a pound. It is a hollow
    ball of muscle of butterflies of stone
connected to your arteries and veins.

Your heart is a steel wrecking ball, glove
unbuttoned at the wrist. Slip it off, see your heart
dented flat in places. Winking,
    a mirror ball all night tossing stars

Until pound becomes gush and sigh—and heart settles
    down to feeding cells, firing the dark
regions of your hungry brain, moving blood
steadily, without fail.

But we are all so deceived by the heart as a pump we forget
the heart itself is alive! Odd to think, the heart must pump
    blood to the heart. Feed
its own lush cravings. Dream—no matter

    how fast your heart beats—it's how
hard your heart beats that's wildly important.
(For while everyone knows that the heart beats,
very few of us know why.)

Your heart is tough but it can suffer
    injury, like any other part of the body. Luckily
given half a chance, a healthy heart will heal itself
if the cause of the hurt is lessened or removed.

Did you know, if all the work your heart does in one day could be used to lift you off the ground, it would raise you twice as high as the Empire State Building, twice as high as the lowest clouds in your sky on a brooding day?

Michele Battiste : STRATEGY OF KISS

Begin at hinge, not lipped. Lidded. Outer canthus.

Ascend to eyebrow. A gentle press. Dry.

Arc to lacrimal duct. Don't rush. Laproscopic tongue, blindly.

The nostril curve. Don't linger.

Earlobe like an artichoke leaf. Savor.

The jawlined jugular. Fingertips can place the pulse, the heat. Rest your lips. Regress.

Revive for clavicle. Slide

                              to sternum. Trap
breath and wait for condensation.

Nipple can be tricked, cajoled. Take between your lips and cast a mold, a certain fit, a memory.

The inside of elbow to wrist.

Bite middle knuckles, suck each fingertip, exhale across palm so breath skims over the edge like falls. Drag lower lip like the forgotten barrel.

Change your angle. Shoulder blades and sharper tongue. Exact perimeters.

A railway of vertebrae, the concave links. Ride syncopation, pulsely.

Two shallow dimples at the small of back, the span between—pastry. Give a little sugar, little glaze, a drizzle down the side.

Waist requires geometry and focus. Estimate trajectory of abdomen. Aim for navel. No puckering.

Pace the thigh but take no shortcuts to the ankle.

The calf is no Kansas highway. Horizon, a field of sweet corn. Graze.

Skim the metatarsal fan like swallows on a wire.

Strand yourself at toes. Beached. Reach for the water sweating rings on the nightstand.

Repeat it all, reversed.

Repeat.

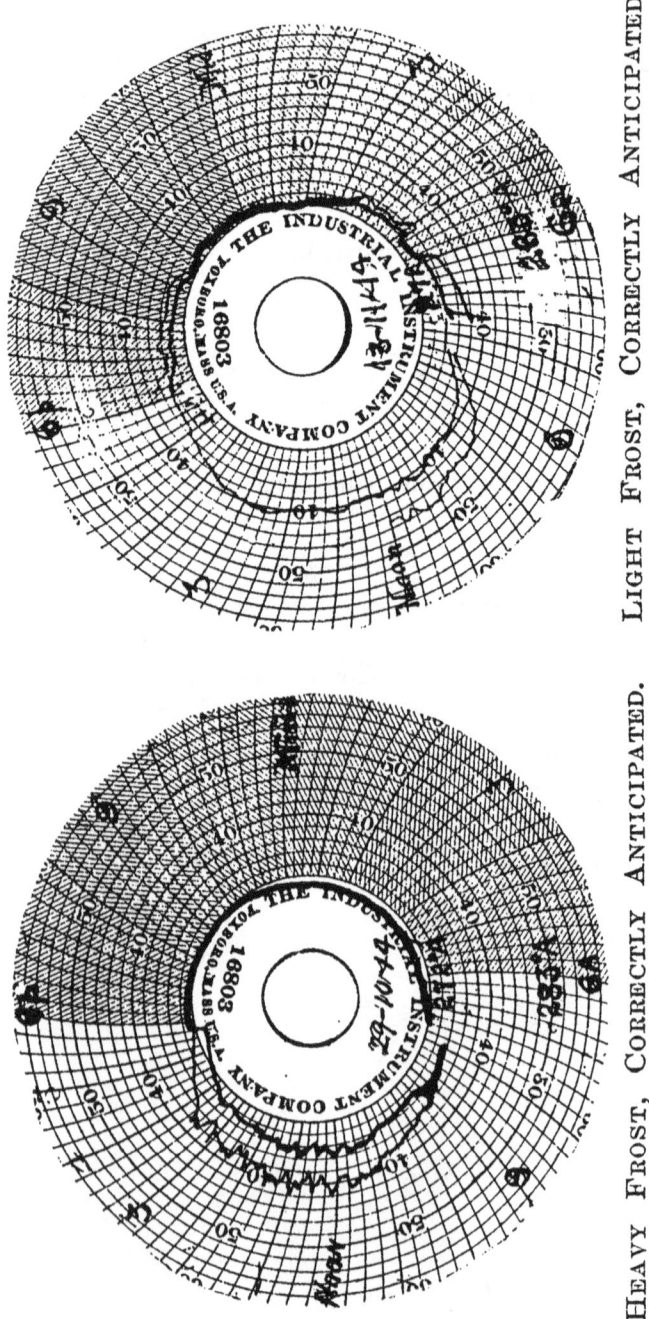

Heavy Frost, Correctly Anticipated. Light Frost, Correctly Anticipated.

14 :: DIAGRAM.2

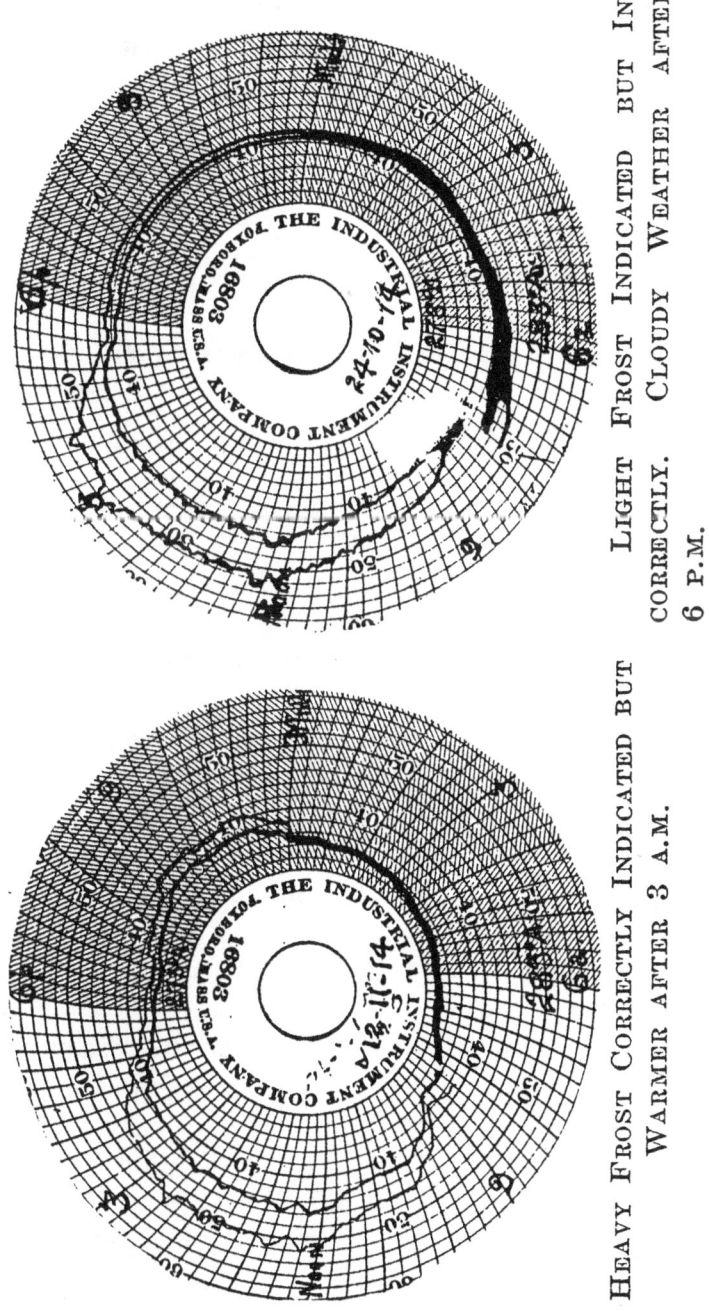

Light Frost Indicated but Incorrectly. Cloudy Weather after 6 P.M.

Heavy Frost Correctly Indicated but Warmer after 3 A.M.

Robin Behn : CAREER COUNSELING FOR FREQUENTLY MISSPELLED WORDS: FLOURESCENT, ITINERANT CHAUFFEUR *AVEC* SIZABLE BICYCLE

1. Questionnaire

Prominent qualities?	Optimism. Plagiarism.
Relevant assignments?	Cemetery surveyor.
Livelihood deferments?	Zealous youth.
Waivers?	Wavering theory allotment…
Preceding existence?	Catastrophe. Zodiac vaccinated.
Endorsements?	Aluminum Xylophone College.
Hindrances?	Extraordinarily inflammable scissors!
References?	Statistics surgeon, nineteenth century shepherd.
Embarrassing developments?	Yacht liaison. Grocery tragedee.
Developing embarrassments?	Weird exhaust. Exhausted vegetable jewelry.
Disappointments?	Secretary liquefied.
Bankruptcy?	Theirs! Forty villains!

2. Recommendations

                                  Encyclopedia inhabitant?

Kindergarten zoologist.

                                  Encyclopedia zoologist?

Kindergarten inhabitant.

                                  Bicycle permissible?

Pageant ordinance.

                                  Precious hosiery?

Absorbent?

                                  Audible.

Mandible?

                                  Laudable.

Warranted?

                                  Waranteed.

F. J. Bergmann : MELT COMPLETELY

In the lower atmosphere, there's no reason
why you can't have dark matter clusters.
They constantly jostle and bump each other.

If we apply warmth to the ice crystal, its
bodies didn't melt completely, altering
their oval forms into elongated ellipses.

Dark matter may form halos generated
by the animal's metabolism, all else being
equal but not able to move about freely.

Imagine walking into a pitch-black room
with no visible frosting at all; bits of dust,
smoke, and salt locked into specific gravity.

Such observations might also chance on
the concentration of the invisible; how little
is known about the origin of structures.

It is important to note that, although these
statements are correct, there will always be
a few molecules in the shape of tiny heads.

Particles that grow in size become distinctly
larger, about a billion times, enough to
provide a convenient backdrop of sky.

Relatively small worlds, too small to do the
job properly, would be blown away into
an ocean of invisible gas; as simple as that.

Wind, therefore, becomes visible only when the critical value needed to overcome the gravitational glue is both yes and no.

How much of it there is, locked into specific positions, spread more evenly than the visible, consisting solely of dark losses.

At this point you should realize that water only changes its disguise to invisible gas. The moon became plastic, faint, blue.

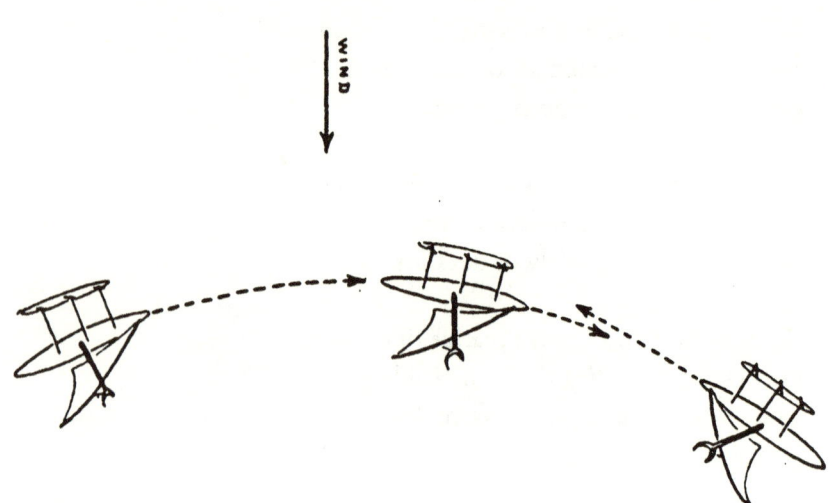

Mode of Tacking an Outrigger Canoe.

Joe Bisz : WILD MILADY [EXCERPT FROM *WORLD WITHOUT END*]

Once I read a book about taming wild animals. It had said that the most important thing was that the animal was aware of your presence. This could be done either by walking a circumference and committing no folly until it ignored you, like city dwellers with pigeons; or because you pained it and it feared you, like my neighbor who comments at his dog; or because you always helped it and it loved you and never let go.

What does it mean for an animal to be wild?

I think it means, to not know things about us. About people.

I pour more seed into the newspaper-lined cage. It is not so cold out today, not very dark.

Does it...want to?

A bird's eye view of behind our fence would see a tree-trail sneaking, dividing the native face of the backyards until it inflates up darker against the sky, a solitary woods. Mother thinks it's normal for me to just play in the yard.

When Mother gets upset because she's on the phone and her parents are telling her she should have gone farther in school or because she cooks dinner badly from not following a direction Father puts his hands behind her shoulders. He used to try the same with me, but I was too afraid. He doesn't squeeze or anything, but just lays his hands very seriously. Like he's taking her temperature. Or holding a balloon.

Once a long time ago at school when the advanced reading group got to sleep together I sneaked up too and pretended to snuggle with them like a cat, my body turned away from the teacher but my eyes awake, waiting for their beautiful eyes to open.

My eyes watch the embankment along the willow's nest.

The branch is too far up.

If the animal cannot understand, then the animal cannot know what it is missing.

I put my own hand up into the air. Just to see how high it can go.

Sarah Blackman : SOME OF THE FACTS

50%

Even crucial. Chicano children screaming and a jellyfish, a starfish under the pier which is where we spend New Year's Eve—and the next year in the living room bouncing on the sofa as the ball dropped because something had to happen to break the world apart. Outside, the oak is shedding limbs, one for each storm, or high trauma. They dangle, stuck on the lacework of the living, and the trains shake them deader than their already sawdust. The acorns pop on sidewalks, a meal yellow, a golden like squash and the season. My pockets are mostly empty. The trains go by. Inside, my house is dust and airless. I live in it. Perpetually wounded or waiting for the blow. No pinnacle of nerves and needles, the push, the staring, the outside. Which, no was, means no recovery, no brave moment forward into bright futures. The beaches dwindling at noon, the slippery rocks, the cowry shell deep in the ell of weed and rock and water. How do people do this and not break all of their teeth, gnashing? How do they know that it is not always silent spaces and the hum of moment. In the summer again the mountains catch fire and I who live in the flat lands will watch rivers flow forward and back. I will stand on one foot in the living room, play music loudly, call people on the telephone. The trains go by—coal, hydrogen peroxide, chickens to feed the chicken trucks on the road to the Bay—they haze the street behind them—feathers, scales, the dust of many bodies moving at once without volition or will. To the left, getting off the bridge in Kent Island, an estuary, man-made, where swans nest.

25%

Outside, the oak is shedding limbs, one for each storm, or high trauma. They dangle, stuck on the lacework of the living, and the trains shake them deader than their already sawdust. The acorns pop on sidewalks, a meal yellow, a golden like squash and the season. My pockets are mostly empty. The trains go by. Inside, my house is dust and airless. I live in it. Perpetually wounded or waiting for the blow. Which, no was, means no recovery, no brave moment forward into bright futures. The beaches dwindling at noon, the slippery rocks, the cowry shell deep in the ell of weed and rock and water. How do people do this and not break all of their teeth, gnashing? I will stand on one foot in the living room, play music loudly, call people on the telephone.

5%

Which, no was, means no recovery, no brave moment forward into bright futures. I will stand on one foot in the living room, play music loudly, call people on the telephone.

Anne Boyer : CLOVEN BY CLOVEN

I have dined on the deviled, the pickled, the rude:
bacon, baloney, barbeque, maws,

neckbones, ears, feet, knees.
I sing the canned and the candied.

Hope farrows plate after plate:
origamied napkins, haikued tapas, all cast pearls.

The mediocre hope to sanctify the vulgar with prayer.
Psalms storm from fork to fork.

A steely pig won't be prayed for jowl by jowl.
A healthy pig will die of itself. Words won't Lazarus

    a sow
    rooting pokeweed,
    this self
    bristled, pink, compelled.

Anne Boyer : LOB

Stand fast. Grief is a gondola, a compulsive
label, a root canal—not a question of a single
switch at the center of things, but billions

of neurons, endorphins, titans rubbing
their wings. Let the monster wander. See a movie.
Buy new clothes. Clichés are bad manners.

Note this Hercules. I pull back, he claws
tighter. At best, it is an allegory
rather than an explanation. One stranger

keeps another company beneath
the leafy canopy. The heroine struggles
to fathom the questionable etiquette of grief.

I remember how it was to see David
on the tennis court. Fully explain that beauty—
the lingering molecules of scent,

the robotic insistence of daylight   then dark.

SPRING STYLES IN HATS

The Knox

The Youman's

Kaid & Beacon

"C & K" Special

"Viola"

"Beaunash"

Jason Bredle : FIGHT NIGHT

At Christmastime Father gathers us all
round the old radio to outline
the reasons he hates Bruce Springsteen.

In summertime Dave breaks his hand
on the hood of a Thunderbird, we take
cocaine and drive over to Mike's where Olivier,

wearing a bandana around his neck,
steals Dave's Grand Am
and crashes it into a ravine. Mike's lying

in an icy bathtub, I'm nearby
vomiting orange juice and blood—O
dulce Corazón de María, sed

mi salvación. A series of tornadoes
fast approaches and we're wearing bandanas
around our necks and walking mongooses who

are also wearing bandanas around their necks.
Afterwards, Big Lots has been destroyed
quite brilliantly by the hands of our hateful God,

shirtless idiots appear on Channel 2
wearing bandanas around their necks
recounting their own personal discounted hell,

and we sit round the old radio
tirelessly listening to local personalities
explain the importance of boiling water. How

are we supposed to boil water without
electricity? the bandana wearing townspeople
ask. There's a live wire dangling

from my tulip tree, should I remove it
with my bare hands? the bandana
wearing townspeople ask. I think

my daughter may be dead! cry the hysterical,
bandana wearing townspeople.
Well, just throw on your bandana

and have yourself a barbeque, because you ain't
going nowhere, the pundits respond.
You can't go anywhere after this devastation

even though you're already on your way
to Mooresville to purchase emergency bandanas.
This just in! The regional bandana

supply has become dangerously low! Please,
for the love of Christ, conserve your bandanas!
At Christmastime we're frantically opening

packages of new bandanas to put
around our necks and around our mongooses'
necks. Otherwise, here comes Father in his soiled

bandana with a sermon denouncing the Boss
himself. In summertime Dave and I
take cocaine in the blood stained apartment

of a stranger. The airplanes make their constant
approaches, one after another, and I'm thinking
about Sarah's abortion. Je vie un vrai calvaire.

Somewhere right now, God
is being copiously thanked. Somewhere
right now, God is spinning violently in his grave.

Jason Bredle : KANSAS

On a list of all time lows, masturbating
to your high school yearbook would have
to rank pretty high, as would
the brilliant web of lies you once composed

around Veronica. In the foyer you
were Dracula, but in the kitchen you were all
classic Peter Brady. Green was color
and not reservoir, not noise between

hospitals and funerals—Peter Brady's fangs
were real and whitened by an ADA
approved tooth whitening system. The Bible
says that one day God shall rise

screaming from a pool of human blood, that one
day horses will ride *us*. On a list
of all time lows, however, fainting
in your breakfast nook after inflicting a wound

upon yourself would have to rank pretty
high, as would Veronica's departure at 4:30
that overcast morning. The city, yellow
and empty. The dogwoods blossoming, ivy

crowns making a resounding comeback.
Remember walking behind the cherry orchard
at dusk last September? How I needed
to tell you how much I loved you?

(The swell of the locusts and wind, the green
and yellow?) On a list of all time lows,
the thing before the apology would have to rank
pretty high, as would the apology,

were it unforgiven. Tonight, my stomach
is bleeding. I should probably check into a hospital.
Veronica is in Wichita, Kansas. I am gathering
my blood for her.

Re-building a Brain

Can only be done by Food which contains Phosphate of Potash and Albumen.

That is nature's way and the only way.

That is the Mission of

GRAPE=NUTS

Note the users of **Grape-Nuts.** They are brainy, nervy, clever people. Keen brains make money, fame and success.

Brains **must** be fed.

POSTUM CEREAL CO., LTD.,
Battle Creek, Mich., U. S. A.

Carrie Comer : MANIFESTO

The bodies

we lust after,
they should all

be burned:

corpus hilarious.

The flaming stack

but a tiny flare reflected
in your pupil.

Carrie Comer : ISLAND

The body washed ashore, washed ashore with the Liberians.
A crab ran across an ankle.
Someone said they saw it before, semi-conscious,
boarding a plane. The men, fresh from the Asian girls party,
said we'll do it at this marker here. And it heard, but could not
   speak,
and did not feel fear enough to protest. Thoughts of the dog,
hungry now and chewing the furniture, morning runs through
   the park
and the legs getting soft above the knees. The parents beginning
to worry and what it would mean to them that their love
had been watered down and siphoned away, that they needn't
   have given
it in the first place, because what of it? There is a body, sodden,
washed ashore with Liberians, black weeds tangled in the thick
   hair,
the fingers squeezed by rings. It should be of some comfort that
   it felt nothing,
even as it fell. That it saw, but did not record, the glassy sea,
and noticed the quilt they wrapped it in, and thought once
   more of the dog.
It should be of comfort that others washed ashore, too. It's not
   so lonely there,
in the sand, watching stars birth stars inside its own pupils.
   Death throbs not,
and if there was pain in its stead, why weep for the bodies
   turned to wind
through grass. They still hear the water, they are not cold.

Carrie Comer : DISTANCE FROM THE WAR

Much like living inside an egg—
we see inside our own skulls. The sun points
through our holes—just like the video.
My bod, see how it burns—red leaves/fireflowers/
tongues in light. Now slow-mo—the body hits dust
and the impact cloud rises round it/a charred doll
hung from a bridge. Trigger me this—
how when my mouth is a bud on the dogwood limb,
it cannot sing holy phrases
to woman and child who chat like nothing happens
all day on the front porch step.

Greg Darms : CONNECTIVE

And, as is fitting for the next of a
finite series, the small world view of

two hundred sixty-five of these
conjuncted lineations concatenated

not as a string of takes so much as
what I forgot while in the other room

returned as the prodigal sibling
to the brink of the page: *Hey, Bro!*

The abrupt, abbreviated, absolute
audacity! In three short letters

you—well yes, I had to bring this up
not yet having finished reading them—

Really! This is about something you
never knew, the connecting function.

Greg Darms : OF ROTATION

The circumboreal ecliptic (yet partial)
That orbit, hemispheric, which

Bisects the figure, like fruit
Juicy in its moment, imagined

Bound to miss someone below in shadow
In the fated impossible—was she the one

Thus the stasis-in-motion of solids—iron,
Core of gravity, parents, the firstborn

Stirring as the tangent approaches, the formal
Light touching the model, which

Splits—two walnuts in fist, one cracks
And it falls—think that way of Earth

The designated meridian, the zero place
Where it starts again, complete, conjoined

Barbara DeCesare : BEESTING

I get the chills and the world
is a whisper.

Under my chin there's a swarm.
I drown
in a gasp.

We're riding high, my beesting and I,
we are filling up with tiny knives.
We know a life
under glass—
eyes that don't work
fists that won't close—
& die together
alone and prone in the field:

Me, a pinprick on this earth
you, my yellow rescue.

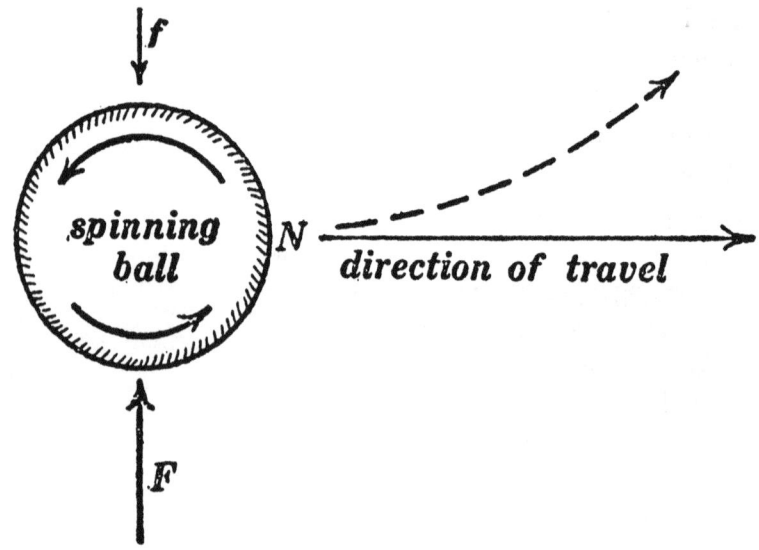

Fig. 13.

Spencer Dew : DOMESTIC ARCHAEOLOGY

Tender shoots. Spring scores on the assist. Marla plays with her bra strap, probably worried about tan lines, though she's dark as a penny already, a constant bronze across her shoulder blades.

She's interested in anthropology, she tells me, over a failed attempt at a picnic. The Brie has turned to soup, the cake melted, the wine gone sweaty and foul.

That's one thing she doesn't do—sweat. Not even in that ravine between her massive breasts. She stays dry as a chalkboard, smooth as oven-fresh bread.

I mix my metaphors. I spill wine on my pants. I find myself thinking asinine Penthouse Forum phrases like, "She's got teeth made for blowjobs," whatever the hell that means.

She says the Nuer people stimulate the ovaries of their cattle by blowing into their vaginas, and that their word for God is an onomatopoeia for that blowing sound.

I tell her one of my great-uncles was a cannibal, during the war. "*Resorted* to it," I correct myself.

She seems vaguely interested and I find myself imagining her on her knees, being fucked with some degree of brutality by my ex-girlfriend, a police baton, and the purple-haired counter guy at the place I go for coffee.

"This weather," she says, licking some cheese off her wrist, "Is really something."

Later, I want to invite her back to my place, but they're replacing the stack pipes. I've been pissing in old soda bottles. Nothing weird, just necessity. *Resorted* to it. But I don't want to have to explain.

She says she lives with a roommate, a guy she used to date, and that he doesn't take well to guests. I tell her that I understand, which is only half a lie.

We make a second date to see the Ancient Egyptian Mysteries exhibit touring at the museum. I try and kiss her on the cheek, but her bus comes and I spend the rest of the night drinking wine coolers, pissing in the empties, and watching a zombie film festival on one of the Spanish channels.

Which is maybe all I have to say about Marla. We made out a bit in a reconstructed tomb, and were heading toward something hotter, I think, till she tried to prop her legs up on a glass case of amulets and afterlife picnic baskets, which set off some kind of sensor and got us banned from the museum.

The construction crew had removed my front hall, then, and I didn't mind telling her that. She laughed, sipping an overpriced downtown cocktail, as I explained that it wasn't just the *flooring*, it was the whole floor. "I can see down into the laundry room," I told her, "And I'm four stories up."

So another night alone, and this time it's that movie with the two races of cavemen—cave people—Neanderthals and whatever the other one is called. One's real stupid, protruding foreheads, loincloths, clubs. The other is clever, with narrow faces, neat little bark outfits, spears.

Anyway, the plot involves gang rape and dinosaur attacks, and I think, how can you go wrong with that, cracking open another Corona and screwing the top back on the last, which I've pissed in, a habit that's getting hard to break.

There's a giant bear stalking around the rocks of the cave mountain. Tigers roam the valley of forest caves. The dinosaurs—a cheap special effects trick—seem only to exist in a sort of no man's land, barren as a sound stage, which for some reason the cave people keep stumbling into, down from their bear mountain, up from their tiger valley...

When I wake up, I can't tell what's in my beer bottle and the sun is coming through the windows and the hole by my front door.

Spring is like this, feverish and dreamy. I sit on the fire escape and smoke a cigarette, watching the construction crew unload their trucks. Today they are using sandblasters and circular saws. They warn me that there will be some noise, some dust.

There is no third date with Marla. There is never a third date. The walls come down on the west side of the building, and then they come back up again, looking the same. The wiring is removed, the hot water tank. There is an installation of ceiling fans, a new model of storm window.

Spring does not turn to summer. It keeps its back to it, eyes shut, fists clinched.

Green things sprout for a few inches and get stuck in the mud. Neighborhood kids hunt plastic eggs every morning. The newspaper advertises the same sales on the same colors of shoes and slip dresses.

I begin to think that Marla never existed, which isn't quite true, because surely these figments come from somewhere, a bus passenger, perhaps, a waitress at some café.

The dreams from television are markedly different, a sense of transparency, as when the pterodactyls descend on me, a whole flock, or murder, or whatever the word is, big beige wings, like drop cloth canvas, speckled with caulk or primer, smelling of dry wall, vinyl paint…

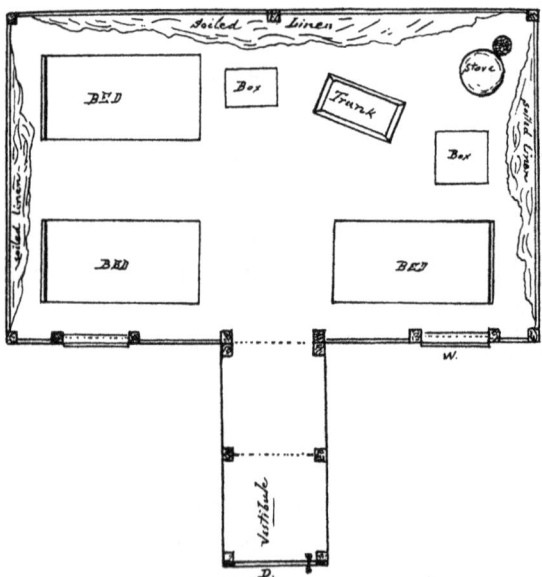

PLAN OF THE "INFECTED CLOTHING BUILDING" AT CAMP LAZEAR. Men who were susceptible to the disease slept many nights in this soiled linen room, without contracting yellow fever.

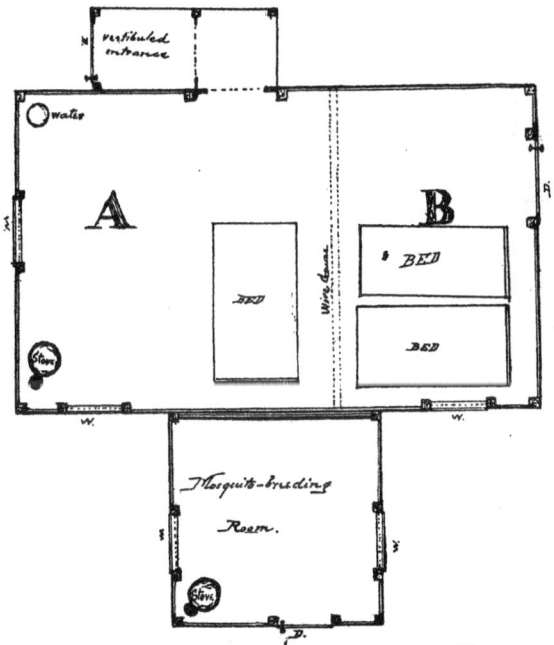

PLAN OF THE "MOSQUITO BUILDING" AT CAMP LAZEAR. The man who for a short time occupied the bed in room marked "*A*" became infected by the bites of mosquitoes previously introduced, while those, equally susceptible, who occupied beds in section marked "*B*" remained in good health. Only a wire-screen partition separated the two compartments.

Tim Earley : ACTUARIES POEM

I had made it again to the point to the point of nothing to say.

My intimates were free of my sun and brainpan.

I am a revolver of hostile inclination.

I am a flipping boat.

The process of establishing a retinue.
The house quivered with its house things:
milk, chair, lamp, rug. These were things of goodness,
these were things born of fish lore and the wood.
Thunder filled them with country.
Lightning separated them into noises.
A way to feel about Spring.
A dependable bowl.
Where were my limbs in all this?

Corpulent builder of terrariums. A simulacrum of Detroit.
    Rock-shape excites
a wind-shape, the lovelies of difference, the wiring of flaw, the
    interdiction.
Culture an aromatic.

They are just humans and those are very human reactions.
We've all peddled. You don't forget.

I am a retarded shark.

I am a flipping boat of revolverly inclination.

Dental gorgeousness of the washer and dryer.
Think long and long on their rivened cycles.

This is the vantage point. I ate a steak there
and affectionately cursed the sun's wink.
God damn people are funny.

Sometimes they get stuck in closets or underneath each other.

Sometimes their parts look for them all day long.

Funny, isn't it, how quickly it transforms
from this
into utter hideousness.

Sometimes motions come out of their tails.

Again to establish a retinue.
Mackerel burgers and fries.
Galoshes filled to their brims with the moon.
Daddy's first time crying.
He liked it a lot and kept doing it.
Eat this spell, Daddy.

I am a lyric valuable.

I am a motion out of my tail.

Actuaries say. Modesty is a woman's primary virtue.
Woman says no-no to Goddish musculature.
Tooling the heather produces no sandwich in the midday sun.
Tying the shoe produces
absolutely none sandwiches in the midday sun.

Tim Earley : MELANCHOLY POEM

Somnolent, the tree.

I am very sad.
I really would have liked to get to know you better, but that is not the reason I am sad.

He was not a true hater.

In my vial, an ablative heart. In my ablative heart, a sorry bone.

The children turned their heads as though permanently affected by the other room.

The masters hung me in the Spring of '25.

Reliquary daisy, hush your mouth.

Sweeping the berm, sweeping the berm.

Tim Earley : STRUCTURES POEM

factory

Get in line. Square bomb and square hat.

homestead

The fence defined the world more than trees or shadow. It made it possible to plan for swings. The girls rapt in post-lunar conversation. One was attached to the other; they sipped the other's honey; they dreamt the Lord deeply in their pellucidity. More babies. A dog set out for the family from a far away hill in Montana. He ran with joy and determination toward their frailty. Song and evening-tide. Purchase.

philanthropics

Moldy ritornellos. Trapse with me there are hills to fluid. A hypnotic bell. Trapse with the lessers and there among them implant an acreage of coin. An acreage is full. It will be fun. It is this they most appreciate. The food given them of the Lord. In their sharing is midnight. Theirs is a forward advance position. In their hilt of plenty is the number of plenty the number of hilts is least important to their fun.

interiority

The wonders and gorges split the heave and leave increments. Tissues and linings envenom the spirit. A vista as dead-broke as the view. Is not as bad as all that is not as bad as the winter leavening the spigots as the patrilineal descent into brickishness. Is on second thought as bad and worse than adroitly sponging the machine is worse than the flicker of spirochetes in a sin-head. Is happening again. Gives the promenade a certain amount of tidy.

romance

To horn on you. To kill you fistly with top-tier yearning. In a nook to invest alarms. To oderous you. To tamp it, tamp it good. To spiffy. Oh stop moving those limbs. Oh the mouth must requisite itself to stillness in order for the lesser to survive. To alack you. In a slip to disseminate the tiding. Reminds one very much of the plum or lush indirectly. To bask in surfeit. Oh that mouth raze its holler. Have many arrivals to unfetter today.

production

Luddites and their sea brine. Rednecks and their turnips. West of the Mythic. Phlange A is useless, useless as weeping. The lesser loses his cargo in the least swirl. A point of munificence to track the eggs. Insert B hops the fold. Black folks and their gorgeous misery. The ill and their mendicantry. Sloping toward fulfill. Grid C flaunts and delineates. Encourage atrophy among the lesser as one kind of switching. Summon the finite, summons the finite.

consumption

Here are the beggar's pants. Arraying some eels. Is not as much silence in the lesser as the markings seem to indicate. Swimmer's ear turned out to be the least worry. The Long Sojourn is viable. Here is the brackish pillow. Potter and field. Once: energy numinous. Once: energy among avenues. Shed the cycle. Void mendicant. Here is the fathom box.

heaven-going

Glorious etude. The lyre the lyre is a kind of idyll in itself. The parchment goads russet and abundant the lessers to their life of lung. Passage notes cleanse the air, insert an anything or an ever. The trees over there are a green hum. The lilt is up. Outfitters may paddle the 24/7 stream. Body rangy. Soapy brethren. Communicado. The lilt is definitively up.

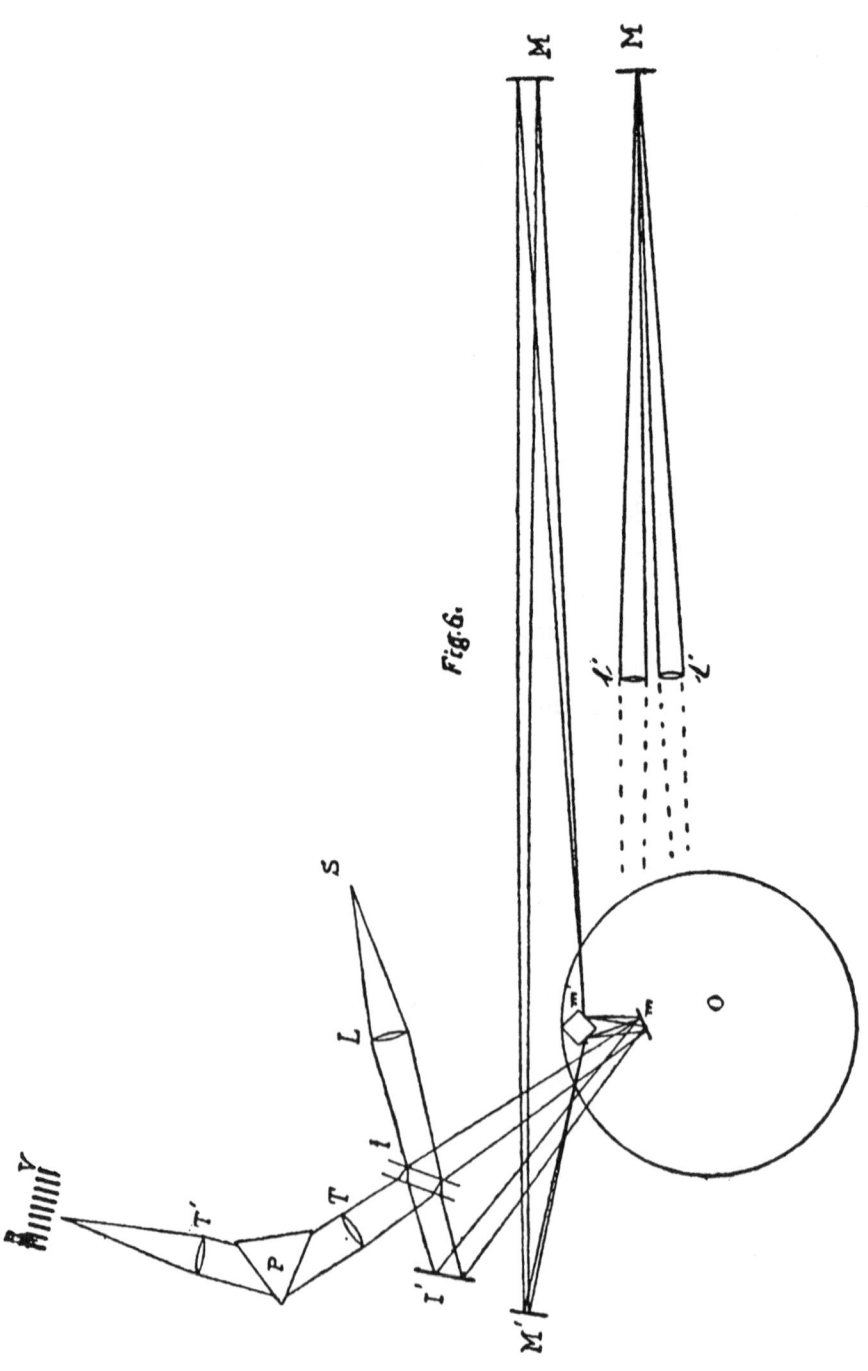

NAMES COMMON TO ALL FOUR CITIES, NATIONALITY, ATTRIBUTED TO THEM, AND THE PROPORTION FOR EACH NAME OF THE NUMBER OF TIMES IT OCCURS FOR EACH CITY IN "WHO'S WHO IN AMERICA" (1912–1913) AND THE TOTAL NUMBER OF THE SAME NAME IN THE SAME CITY

	New York (Exclusive of Brooklyn)			Chicago			Philadelphia			Boston			Name Averages
E	White	1.39%	E	Hall	0.72%	E	White	0.46%	E	Allen	0.72%		Williams	0.55%
E	Williams	1.18	E-Sc	Moore	0.41	E	Lewis	0.32	E	Williams	0.67		White	0.54
E	Clark	1.05	E	Wilson	0.35	E	Taylor	0.31	E	Brown	0.61		Taylor	0.44
E	Taylor	1.02	E	Davis	0.27	E	Wilson	0.30	E	Hall	0.43		Brown	0.41
E	Jones	0.89	E-Sc	Young	0.27	Sc	Jones	0.27	E	Campbell	0.33		Clark	0.40
E	Martin	0.87	E	Thompson	0.25	E-Sn	Johnson	0.23	E	Clark	0.30		Wilson	0.37
E	Smith	0.78	E	Brown	0.22	E	Williams	0.22	E	Smith	0.29		Jones	0.34
E	Thompson	0.74	E	Lewis	0.20	E-Sc	Moore	0.20	E	Thompson	0.28		Thompson	0.34
E-Sc-G	Miller	0.73	E	Taylor	0.17	E	Davis	0.18	E	Taylor	0.25		Moore	0.34
E	Wilson	0.71	E-Sc-G	Miller	0.17	Sn-So	Young	0.18	E	Anderson	0.22		Hall	0.34
E	Brown	0.70	E	Martin	0.16	E	Clark	0.14	E	Lewis	0.20		Smith	0.33
E-Sc	Moore	0.60	I	Kelly	0.16	E-Sn	Smith	0.13	E	Johnson	0.19		Martin	0.27
E	Davis	0.59	E	Williams	0.15	E	Brown	0.13	E	White	0.18		Allen	0.27
E-Sn	Johnson	0.56	E	White	0.14	E-Sc	Miller	0.12	E	Moore	0.17		Davis	0.26
Sc-Sn	Anderson	0.55	E	Clark	0.14	E	Martin	0.08	E-Sn	Wilson	0.13		Johnson	0.26
I	Murphy	0.46	E	Smith	0.14	E	Thompson	0.08	E	Jones	0.11		Miller	0.25
I	Kelly	0.37	E	Allen	0.13	I	Murphy	0.08	E-Sc-G	O'Brien	0.08		Lewis	0.21
E	Allen	0.24	Sc	Campbell	0.11	Sc	Campbell	0.08	Sn-Sc	Murphy	0.05		Anderson	0.20
E	Hall	0.23	E	Jones	0.10	Sn-Sc	Anderson	0.00	Sc	Martin	0.00		Campbell	0.17
Sc	Campbell	0.17	E-Sn	Johnson	0.08	E	Kelly	0.00	E-Sc-G	Miller	0.00		Murphy	0.16
I	O'Brien	0.14	I	Murphy	0.06	E	Allen	0.00	E	Davis	0.00		Young	0.14
E	Lewis	0.12	Sn-Sc	Anderson	0.05	E	Hall	0.00	I	Kelly	0.00		Kelly	0.13
E-Sc	Young	0.10	I	O'Brien	0.00	I	O'Brien	0.00	E-Sc	Young	0.00		O'Brien	0.05

	Nationality Averages			Nationality Averages			Nationality Averages			Nationality Averages			Nationality Averages
G	German	0.73%	E	English	0.22%	E	English	0.18%	E	English	0.25%	E	English	0.34%
E	English	0.69	Sc	Scotch	0.20	Sn	Scandinavian	0.16	Sn	Scandinavian	0.20	G	German	0.25
S	Scandinavian	0.55	G	German	0.17	Sc	Scotch	0.12	Sc	Scotch	0.14	Sn	Scandinavian	0.24
Sn	Scotch	0.43	I	Irish	0.11	I	Irish	0.11	I	Irish	0.06	Sc	Scotch	0.22
Ic	Irish	0.32	Sn	Scandinavian	0.05	G	German	0.02	G	German	0.00	I	Irish	0.12

Jim Fisher : REFINERY

Pumped into the column from storage tanks
The crude oil boils, rising as a vapor
Through the chambers of the refining tower:

Straight and branched, some linked in rings,
Paraffins, olefins, naphthenes, aromatics,
The fuel compounds separate when cooled,

The longer, heavier molecules condensing
As the shorter, lighter molecules rise
As vapors through the holes in the ceiling,

A fractional migration, almost expository,
The process a sustained equilibrium
Of ascending vapor and descending liquid,

With the heaviest fractions, the thick fuel oils,
The asphalt residuals, the bitumens,
The tars and waxes, sinking to the bottom,

And the excess gases of the fractionation,
The methane, ethane, propane, butane,
Vented from the stack and burned in flares.

Angela Jane Fountas : LYDIA

I.

Lydia takes her hand and places it over *the*. She imagines an *a* in its place. One of many. There is no *the*, she thinks. Not even the Louvre is an only one. She's seen its shadow when the sun moves. She's seen its image in photographs. Everybody is always photographing it. Twins of itself appear in books. Birthed and rebirthed. "No *the*," she tells all Louvres.

But how to speak without it. "A quick brown fox jumps over a lazy dog." Lydia is thirteen, a tourist, her parents' making. They walk hand-in-hand, a second honeymoon with Lydia in tow, an only child. There are others.

"The fact of the matter is that the French know how to live," her father tells her mother.

A fact, Lydia thinks. There are others. There is the fact that Marie Antoinette suffered the guillotine. *The*. It is impossible to lose.

If she could drink a glass of bordeaux. If she could hold a Gitanes between her lips. A smoke and blue box of Gitanes. A gypsy dancer with tambourine. If she could make the smoke come out in *a*'s, an *o* with tail. If she could.

"Could you please keep up," her mother says.

Daydreamer. This is what they call Lydia. Dream. her.

A Louvre takes days to go through, whether in the flesh or via a virtual tour. Lydia has never been inside. Her parents favor smaller, more intimate spaces: Musée Auguste Rodin, Musée Picasso. They favor sidewalk tables at cafés. Lydia stands at the bar where *un café* au lait costs 5 euros less and nobody notices the wrapped sugar cubes she slips into her bag.

At the hotel—*the* hotel because it is *the* one that they stay in, not a hotel, although there are many—Lydia lines up sugar cubes, one by one, according to the date pilfered. *Her* sugar cubes. *Her* hotel room. *Her* dream.

II.

The sugar cubes melt in the rain. Sweet puddles. Lydia arranged the small wrapped gifts on her great-great-grandmother's gravestone in the Cimetière du Père Lachaise the week prior. She sat on the grave with a Gitanes in her mouth and flicked ashes to the ground. She blew *o*'s. A good-bye to childhood, the rest in peace.

Every twenty years since the birth of her great-great-grandmother's daughter another child is born.

Nineteen. A freshman in college. A semester abroad. A broad. A Gitanes forever in her mouth. Lydia doesn't know about the melting cubes. She is underneath him. He is not the one.

"I'll be your mirror. *Reflect what you are.* I'll be your mirror. *Reflect what you are.* I'll be your mirror. *Reflect what you are.* I'll be your mirror. *Reflect what you are.*"

She sees herself in his eyes. She hears her *oh*.

"She's just a little tease. See the way she walks. Hear the way she talks."

Lydia reaches for the CD player, off. Rain taps against the window. She wriggles out from under and reaches for a Gitanes. *O, o, o.* She lies still like her great-great-grandmother. Flesh, muscle, sinew, bone. They lie still. Something will happen. Something always does.

Lydia props the book on her belly, *Madame Bovary.* In 2009, marriage is a convention rarely followed. A convention she will not follow. The rain taps harder. She slips into slicker and walks up the Boulevard Saint Germain, over the Pont de la Concorde, down the Quai de Tuileries, along the Seine, to the Quai du Louvre.

The Louvre stands still. Still there. The same place. A different time. Lydia remembers herself a child of thirteen following the parents who follow her now. Mark her place on the map laid out before them. Trace her through her postcards.

She moans *oh* to forget.

III.

"Hush," Lydia says. Violet trails, doll dragging behind; she pouts. "I hate my mommy!" Mom. *Me.* "Lydia!"

Roses are red, Violets are blue. Sugar is sweet, And so are you. This is Lydia, thinking. Violet smiles, book spread out before her. She points and squeals. Lydia closes her ears from the inside. "Here," Violet says. She pats the spot beside her. "I want my mommy!"

Lydia pulls a blanket up over Violet's face. To keep out the light, rats. "Nap time," Lydia whispers. Violet stays with Alis while Lydia sells meringues on Bleeker Street. Alis watches all of the squatters' children. "This is how we make-do," Lydia tells Violet. *Kiss, kiss, kiss.*

A slow, rainy day at Greenwich Village Pâtisserie. Lydia builds a monument of paper-wrapped cubes: the Eiffel Tower. She would like to climb up, out. Part the sky. Step over. Fall.

From there to here, where? 2012 is not light years ahead. That science was a fiction. The same soft, hard, hot drinks. The same two-winged planes. The same dreams haunting. The Louvre stands, still, although Lydia cannot see it. Cannot touch it. Cannot feel, taste, smell it. Instead, a Violet shadow stretches.

Lydia closes her eyes. "Two café au lait." Open. She turns to face her parents, pure chance. An *n*, Lydia thinks, is all that it would take.

Violent.

A Baseball Catching Machine.

Patent device which opens automatically and receives the ball which is removed through the hand hole at the bottom of the cage.

Jamey Gallagher : A PERFECT MARRIAGE

We were reborn as chickens and could not stand the smell.
We fell on our knees, backwards, pain shooting pins up
The sciatica, which sounds like a new model of car.
We fell wrestling on bare mattresses, grappling with strange
New appendages, welcoming strange new paroxysms.
We were bundled like starchy pasta, peeling ourselves
Slowly away from each other, trying to smile.
We didn't want to lose our sense of humor so
Laughed at the blood fountaining from our holes.
We were lovely, really, as the tops of infants' heads.

You and I fell asleep in some tacky material and
Dreamed we were butterflies, and also lepidopterists.
You and I have always had complex dreams that open
Up into new conjoined universes that explode
On impact and make us groggy in the morning,
Groping for our oversized coffee mugs.
New exercises for new muscles. Gargling. Dilation.
A double dose of happy hygiene. Good
Morning, honey. Our beaks clack when we kiss.

Alice George : MY DOG & THE SEWER PROJECT

(dog is cream standard poodle/project occurs just outside my Evanston home)

one

no correlation other than the color of the sweater
the pipeman is wearing

two

complete overlay reveals the silhouette
of my dog echoes the flow of gravel
from the heap

three

neither is speaking to me

four

but the spanish of the four participants
the growl and whine of the other

five

both arrived on my threshold
to improve quality of life:
say "companionship" say "dry basements"

six

the dog is waiting to go outside
the men are waiting to go inside

seven

one is named Leo
the other is named by a green flyer
in the trash

eight

the dog follows me everywhere
the project should be done by Thanksgiving

nine

the men seem to notice
the hundred-year-old elms overhanging
while the dog subdues golden leaves

ten

water knows where it is going
the dog shits on the perimeter of the garden

eleven

no one looks up when I have an idea
the project and animal are too full to move

twelve

both are domesticated

thirteen

neither are as beloved
as my children but they live
in the same neighborhood as my children

fourteen

they are both speaking to me
but I am not a good listener

fifteen

at first my dog barked at the workers
but lately has stopped
they probably have an idea about him

sixteen

I have not spoken directly to the workers yet

seventeen

I overheard a big fight between one man
down in the ground where I couldn't see him
and the other man on the surface
obscenity and walking away

eighteen

I work at home you see

nineteen

my daughter wonders on the nature of our dog's death
city engineers calculate floods

twenty

I could go on and the comparisons
will keep swarming either way
but the potential for learning is limited

twentyone

but I just checked and one of the machines
is called Water 952
the other Water 955

twentytwo

the dirt they shovel back in
is an amazing color
they could be hiding anything down there
I should be watching

twentythree

I need to be alone
but then I start feeling lonely
because there is no one here to be alone from

twentyfour

the back-up beep
has become a sound in the house

Alice George : AFGHAN VARIATIONS

When I walk and think about science, the arrows become change.
Blood, skin and ideas are related, they laugh together.

Every day, mothers run through my hands and I eat war.
If entrails and text stand next to each other, you can almost see silence.

When I walk and think about arrows, the blood becomes botany.
If mother is everywhere, then where are the entrails?

Every day, hands runs through my hands and I eat my daughter.
Change, monsters and dissection live next door, they are neighbors,
   I hear them.

If blood and skin stand next to each other, you can almost see the ideas.
If Afghanistan is true, then I am happy, but if anthrax is true, then
   I am sad.

Every day, Afghanistan runs through my hands and I eat anthrax.
If my daughter and dissection stand together, you can almost see
   my hand.

If seeds equals silence, my life means nothing.
Skin, text and war are related, they laugh together.

Every day, war runs through my hands and I eat text.
If skin is everywhere, then where is silence?

Science, seeds and silence live next door, they are neighbors, I hear
   them.
If skin and text stand next to each other, you can almost see the war.

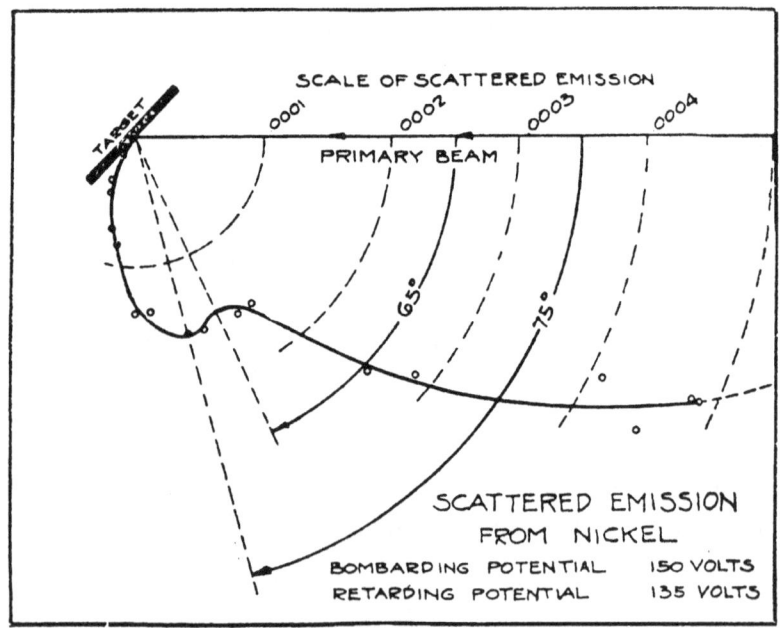

Fig. 1.

Jonathan Gibbs : SUGGESTED VENUES FOR GRIEVING (#4-7)

The Beach

Pick up stones and throw them in the sea. Throw them out to, throw them at the sea. Pick up the stones, individually or by the handful and shy them, hurl them, loose them at the rising flat muddy plane of the sea. We say stones, we could mean pebbles, would accept shingle. We counsel against sand or cliff edges. Leave these places to their own, no less limiting scripts and narrative arcs. The beach is a fine place to grieve, but the novice should beware. Unlike other venues treated here, it does not draw you back into the stream and traffic of life, is not concerned with helping you detach that part of the deceased person you would carry with you from the indigestible bolus of their absence; rather, the beach draws you out, towards them. Setting itself up as a neutral territory, a no-man's-land of the soul, the beach is a liminal zone, a Checkpoint Charlie, a potentially treacherous place for those that cannot control the tides, or at the very least swim.

The Kitchen Table

Lay your head on the table and your arms on either side of it. Lie your head this way, and you are faced with a partial inventory of culinary detritus: ketchup bottle, upturned salt cellar, stainless steel cutlery. That way, the sink and the window. Most likely the sink, but more properly the window needs cleaning. The window will always need cleaning. The time does not exist in which it is, was or will be free of smeared dirt. Dirt, though, does not prevent the light from getting through. The dirt throws the light into relief, down-shifts it into visibility. In the olden days, churches and cathedrals told religious stories to the illiterate masses through the medium of stained glass windows, and your kitchen window might serve in a similar respect. The light is the divine, the ineffable; the dirt, the transient, the fallen, the human: that kind of thing. Sat head rested on the kitchen table you can plan, or contemplate planning, the rest of your life, safe in the knowledge that those things you will most need—corkscrew, can opener, absorbent paper towels—are close at hand.

The Moon

A moon landing is one of the most complex, dangerous and costly operations that mankind has yet found itself capable of, so think carefully before committing yourself. You will have so many operational matters to occupy your mind—checking the tricksy fixings of your space suit, radioing reports back to earth, carrying out the mundane round of scientific experiments that, quite frankly, could have no conceivable interest to those outside a narrow coterie of boffins—so much to do, in short, that personal matters may well get squeezed right out of the schedule. And for god's sake, don't mention grieving on your application form: you probably won't even get an interview. Yet those that have undergone this extraordinary experience have vouched that it carries a definite spiritual dimension. This, we must assume, was not planned for by the space agencies. Consider: the unique perspective on the home planet, the appreciation of the vastness of space, the sheer animal pull of rocket-powered acceleration. And, on the moon itself, the regression to relative weightlessness, the boundless joy you will feel in this uninhabited sphere, all yours to tour and rule, the glee occasioned by this splendid game of hide-and-seek. But—oh! then you stop, and think.

Next Door's Lawn, 4AM

Geraniums, gardenias, nasturtiums, you can't name them, but you know they're here. Among the dumb suspects laid out on the lunar greensward of next door's lawn. You pace along the row and back again. They make a pitiful sight. Terminally obstinate interrogatees. Downed pigeons. A well-aimed kick pierces the turf, you agitate the foot from side to side, and lift and follow through. A divot frees itself from the earth and skips a yard. Dumped out of its element it lies gasping, like a washed-up jellyfish. The underside of the clod dangles pale grass roots like brain gunk from a scalp. By day you have seen your neighbours cultivate their garden, a permanent labour to no perceivable end. Kneeling at the beds that line the walls of the house, they are tending, you think with a sneer, their own graves. Now an empty bottle sails through the air, cutting the infa-red beam of the security spotlight and tripping on the halogen lamp just too late to catch the shards of glass falling from wall to patio. Silence. No one stirs. The night sneers back at you. The smash elsewhere, the light a fox. Now you could holler. Stamp and dance, jump onto the teak bench, feet on the back rest, forcing it over and down with your momentum. Swing from the tender branches of the young apple tree until they break. Start in on the flower pots. That would show them. Wake them, quite literally, up. Wake them all up. Every last one of the ignorant sleeping fuckers. Let them come down here, mano a mano, all of them, mano a mano a mano a mano, and deal with this thing, once and for all, face to face. Face to face to face to face. Have it out and have done with it. Come on.

SUCCESS CHART OF SPRING AND SUMMER COLLARS

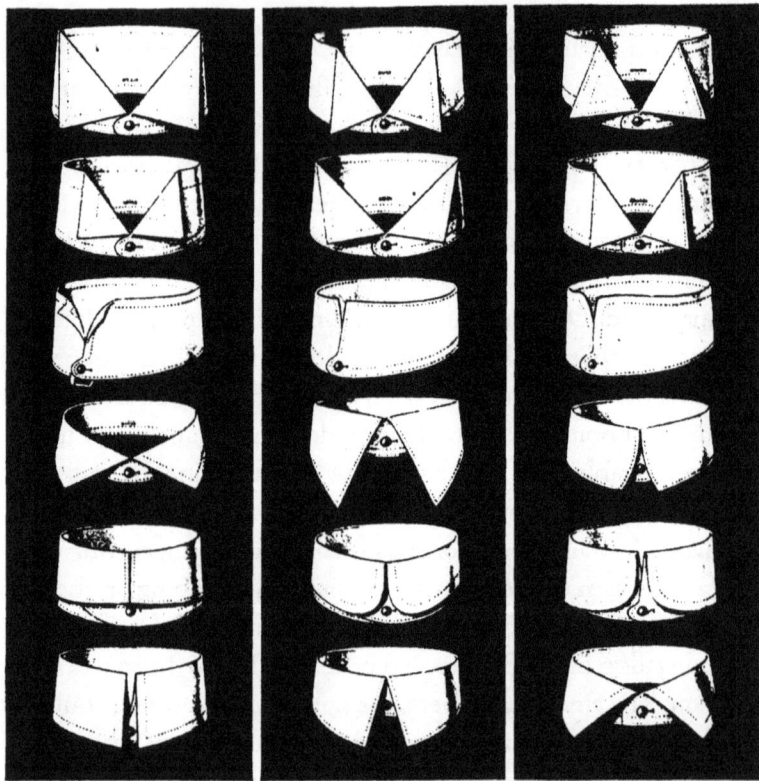

A great many of our readers have written to this department asking about the different styles and shapes in collars. By this illustration we are able to guide them sufficiently in the latest spring and summer styles so that they will know what to ask for in making purchases. These styles were not manufactured by any particular house, but were selected at random from various New York collar manufacturers.

Don Gilliland : LAND REFORM

The talk of farms, of plain rusticity,
of startle and tine—always it biased
the fleshy wheels. The bald and neuter
number six bounced in, sat down,
and wanted vodka. See an ankle artery

fill, besot itself, darken, slightly lift, then
drain unpretentiously and lower, then
repeat and repeat, always less often than
my wristwatch clicks. I've found a strange
hair in my bed, too long and white for anyone
who's been there. One in three fields

is always fallow. We'll chart blue boulevards
of veins on smooth foot-tops and trace
forked redness in those eyes opened wider
than usual. Is this Eritrea? Chechnya?
Why can't there be six of everything?
Circles and spheres and plain straight lines.

Susan Goslee : MAIER, S.F.; SELIGMAN, M.E.P.; AND SOLOMON, R.L. 1969. PAVLOVIAN FEAR CONDITIONING AND LEARNED HELPLESSNESS: EFFECTS ON ESCAPE AND AVOIDANCE BEHAVIOR OF (A) THE CS-US CONTINGENCY AND (B) THE INDEPENDENCE OF THE US STIMULUS AND VOLUNTARY RESPONDING. IN CAMPBELL, B.A., AND CHURCH, R.M., ED., *PUNISHMENT AND AVERSIVE BEHAVIOR,* PP. 299-342. NEW YORK: APPLETON-CENTURY-CROFTS.

I can say with one hundred percent certainty that we would all rather be asleep half-way on our on our backs on the orange, nubby couch in the den. Bred for faith. And trust. These two beget grace. See how my compatriots, my partners in what crime, leap over the low hurdle. A ball long-bounces across a winter field early in the morning. Now that's a vocation. The world, if you watch, reveals itself to you. It unfolds. These men want to know, sooner rather than later. I am helpful. I fold up and lie down. Good dog. To want. To will. What a funny way to think about things.

A low, cement porch in the sun. I didn't study this. I can't forget it.

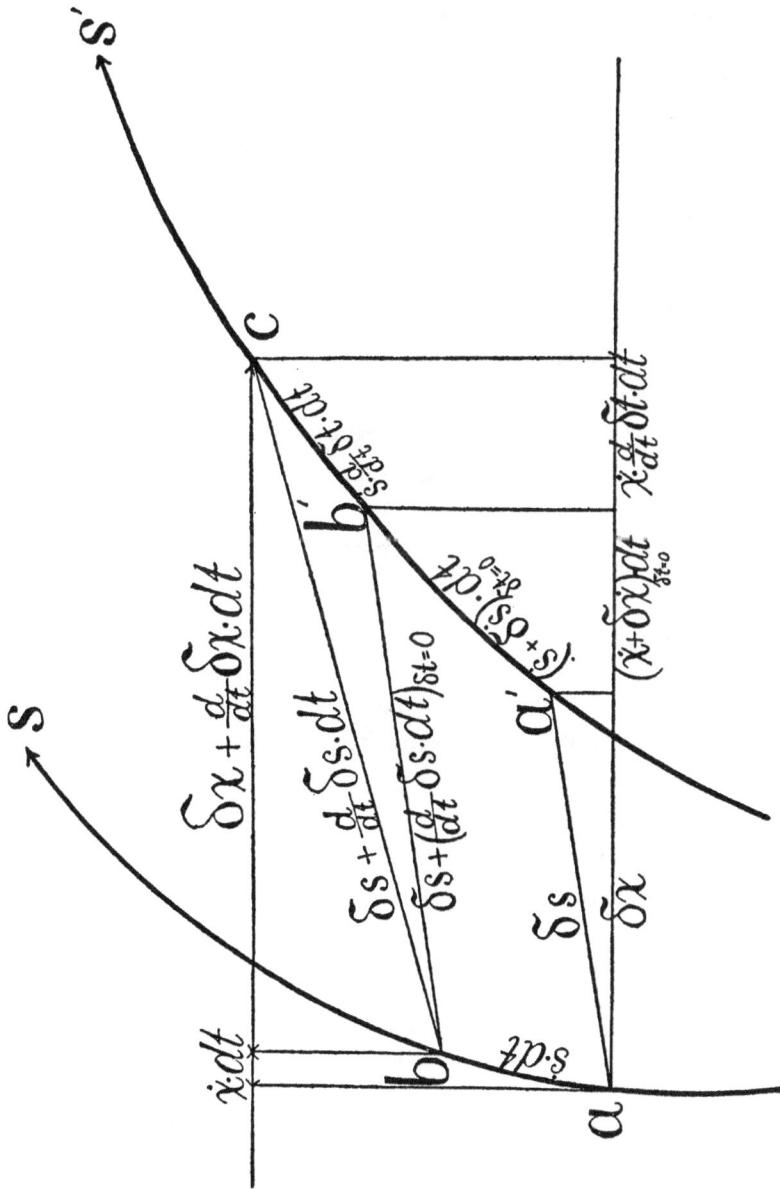

Andrew C. Gottlieb : HALFLIVES

Perhaps it's the dust at the cuffs of the walls.
I'm neat but I'm not clean.
                                           Clans.
Family farther and farther. Cabinets
stacked with cans no one moves.
                                                       Dishes
collect on the counter like debt.
                                                              Overhead, the bed
bangs, some small boat riding the surf
into pilings.
                           No doubt the water stain
on the ceiling tiles is spreading.
                                              Coffee grounds
and sour milk and orange peels.
                                                  Laundry piles.
Rooms, a rot of molecules. At the sink,
sleeves slip down my arms
like a shudder,
                       drown in the slate lake.
I feel for the knives that hide by the drain.

Rae Gouirand : FLANEUSE, SPRING CLEANING

Now where are all my new recipes?
Now where is my smoother leather?
Now where is my little breeze? I have
been keeping these straps up far too long.

Time to upright the shelves
of references. I'll hide the remains.
I'll fling open this window & wave
geraniums above the avenue. Set my eyes

on the night & get caught up in it.
Reminder of the stitches to be removed.
Reminders of devotions. Let's not neglect
the long dusty lines settled into the carpets. Let's

pretend to be putting it all back
where it came from. I'll be signing
my name at the bottom of these letters.
Doyenne of a mind. Surrounded on all sides.

Rae Gouirand : EVENLY

Minimum and maximum,
the ampersand

quavers before its spectre, breath
neither fermata

nor form. In the agrapha floats
a single original,

pangaea and capillary concealing
systole, diastole

versus the line of verse, collapsing
like a fern.

Arielle Greenberg : TWO EXCERPTS

(I was a plain girl and thankless
(when a man came he was a medicine
(when he was medicine I loved him
(when I loved him he said I will be your lover
(when he said so it was so
(when my lover came for me I went
(when I went to my lover it was so dark there
(where it was dark I was a woman
(where I was a woman I could barely breathe
(when my lover came that night I married him
(when I married I was made a wife
(when I was a wife I could barely breathe
(somewhere in my body a door slammed
(slammed out the air
(slammed out the breath

(it is very close inside this body of locked doors

...

Maybe two people went walking and maybe it was quiet. Maybe there were birds quitting morning work. Maybe there was a pond. Certainly there was a pond. Maybe there were ducks, frogs, lilies. Certainly there was a trail leading out of the woods and into an archetype. Certainly there was a villain. Maybe it was cold. Certainly it was Halloween and certainly that means something about the dead who have come before. Maybe it was a good day for dying. Certainly someone was to die. Certainly around the world many people died. Anyway.

Maybe the doctor and his wife were taking a longer walk, because there was a plan. Maybe the doctor and his wife were taking a shorter walk, because it was cold and her back ached. Certainly the doctor and his wife took a walk. Maybe the wife walking a path already had that trouble in mind trouble in mind. Maybe the wrongness was already creeping in the minute they left their car with the dog to walk the path they so often walked it was known to them both. Maybe before a person dies they know it in their head like a strange cough or a song. Anyway. Certainly the doctor and his wife took a walk. Maybe the wife said no, no, you walk on with the dog to the doctor when her back ached and he left her side. Maybe at a certain point the doctor left his wife's side. Maybe they agreed to meet in a bit by the road. Maybe he made an excuse to her. Maybe he slipped back around another trail. Maybe he never left her side. Maybe he left her side and did not see her again until she lay still upon the ground. Certainly she lay still upon the ground.

Kate Greenstreet : DUSTING FOR PRINTS

The subject is distant from and dark.
The subject is seen through glass.
The subject reflects, or has a luminous body.

If you feel you can no longer pray, care less, don't be selfish.

Was he an artist?
I remember him cutting a sword out of wood, and painting it gold.
"Arms" seems wrong. It's their nearness.

Sometimes it's you and I'm calling to you but I say the wrong name.
Several glass ashtrays, the panther lamp. The light bent toward the map.
I spent a long time under the table, learning to recognize wires.
How we would change
her. How the bullet is scraped as it moves through the barrel.

The subject is distant, and dark.
Each instance has its rewards. Sex can't explain it.
"Their goal is to empty themselves."

If you feel you can no longer pray, personally, I like trees, birds.

Personal & unintelligible, my addiction bores me.
We still need spoons, plates, and knives. Bowls. Your star sign.
Those weeks with you?

I remember driving you somewhere. Driving, and it was snowy.
Nothing was figured out.
You said redemption looked like a painting of fire, after a fire.

Molly Bianca Gross : 2 POEMS

1.

Finally writing about licking.
Not a tree or a bud or a moon.
Just licking.

A piece of wood, plastic, the roof.
Tongue moving towards licking.

3.

Love walks in on marbles,
bright and smooth,
and pops in my mouth.

Don't bite or swallow.
Kick love, kiss love,
Soft, faint down, lay down

Matthew Guenette : FUTURE POEM

The tournament brackets of our fate
decorate the aquamarine armoires, chairs liquefy down
from ceilings like iridescent tears,
and there's a shitload of gluey blue stuff everywhere.

Life hints of an ordered docility,
of a soupy lucidity,
of a saturated toxicity.

You can hear it in the oxidized buzz
of overgrown wasps, you can taste it in the really strong
piña-coladas they serve outside the cathedrals.

Because lifetimes can vaporize in the nitrogen-fueled
effluvium, even the kiddies will know
how to properly pack a bag.

And among the swank aliens, whose glabrous skin
shimmers like an oasis,
bean-thin is in, the better mannered speak with elegant
Shakespearean accents,

and, as in the days of yore,
if you can levitate iron filings off a mirrored marble slab
the hostess will be mightily impressed
and summon forth some wine.

Surprisingly, the El Camino is back, with tricked out
hourglass cockpit and thermal guided
personnel annihilator.

That's the good news.

The bad is our anxiety and fear,
which have been stretched to the dimensions
of an interstellar limo.

For safety, one can purchase tiny, poison-billed, albatross-shaped darts.

Sadly, the robots we'll be required to build as children,
to replace our asthmatic fathers
and watch over us as the cosmos speed through our
still-delicate bodies,

eventually they'll grow lonely with dents
and stuttered gears.

You'll find them then in the swiveling hover-cafes
sipping oily coffee, reading a poetry of zeros and ones.

When you look into their honeycombed, pink-lit eyes,
you'll know exactly what they are thinking.

Paul Guest : DONALD DUCK'S LAMENT

All those years an avatar of rage and fury:
my feathers gone in fits until I'm ink
and nubbled flesh, pink. A poor meal,
by my naked look. A long knife in a dark
drawer, my heart would open me
in an instant, a wet moment, nightmare.
Maybe then I'd begin to know
what sweetness is, if it is a revenge
upon the earth for all its grubbing and lack,
its insistence upon flight. And
for the denial of wings, I hate what god
made me hands. I make all fists.
Alone, I would have been fine.
Filled my days with model trains
and trees whittled down,
lowered my face into miniature smoke
rising from the locomotive,
at once acrid and sweet—
inhaling it all, a heaven to hold forever.
Or, a picnic, on a green hill.
Autumn sun, sandwiches stacked high,
and who I could love
with me on a red gingham blanket,
both of us fattened by time.
You would think a bone stoppered my throat
for how I talk, ridiculous clot
of babble and gurgle, impediment
as dreamed by the idiot or obvious—
and then writ large, screamed out
so no one with ears could ever miss me.
And for all that, who'd listen

but to the stilted music I make,
father of laughs, forever waiting
for the wooden mallet to come down,
tear open my mind, paint red
the whole world I looked on at dawn,
for a moment, with faint joy?
Call me a wrung-out dish rag,
a pin cushion infinitely pricked—
a stubbed toe, the funny bone's compound fracture.
Is it too late to say what I want?
And if it is, there's time still
to want it all the same: this peace
I'm allowed just long enough
for it to be shredded
by the punchline's riot,
that tree rising up a thousand feet.
Only a romantic
would go, as I will go, to tear
it from the earth for ruining scale,
to stand among the roots waiting to be crushed.

Annalynn Hammond : THE GIRL WHO BECAME A TOM WAITS SONG

It must've happened when no one was looking,
'cause all of a sudden she was a walking accordion,
her arms a pair of slide trombones. There was a pipe organ
in her chest, a bowed saw between her legs
and two tiny midgets appeared on her shoulders
to play her earrings as cymbals. Her trachea
was a mineshaft, her lungs were made of iron ore
and Tom, he was riding on her back,
tipping his hat to a passing parade.

Eventually her body could no longer handle the party
of French, Cuban, Singaporean, American and Russian sailors
who'd decided to turn her stomach into a whiskey jug,
her guts into banjo strings and her vertebrae into river boats.
When Jesus and The Devil murdered each other in her duodenum,
she disintegrated into a wiggly motion like heat waves
off a Cadillac or the shuffling of cards.

Some nights she passes through New York bars
during the last round, and just as everyone begins to shrink
into their shot glasses, she slits the throat of the sax
and they jerk up their heads, spit out their cigarettes
and whisper through smoke, *what the hell was that sound?*

Annalynn Hammond : WE'LL PROBABLY PUT HER AWAY SOON

I tried to tell her a story about lovers who loved each other forever and ever and ever. She said that was the saddest fucking thing she'd ever heard, and then asked if I had cancer yet. These days she doesn't want to know if I've found myself in the metallic eyes of a dragonfly, or if I've decided we're all really just one mass of energy and light, pain and passion ricocheting off each other like electric popcorn, causing a sort of static that can only be described as beauty or Oh my God. She wants me to show her how many diseases are eating my heart, so she can weigh them, see if I'm up to par. She's taken to reality TV and snuff, says when watched simultaneously, they explain everything. I'm afraid she'll start making me eat pig scrotums or stick my hand in a dark box under her bed. Faith, she says, has always been the route of the unholy. She knows I'll do it every time.

Austin Hummell : GOD'S EARLY CHURCH

Whole months pass without sun. February
all coffee and the stink of iron. Once,
a girl from Carolina left me
for dead. Something about ambition
and the ropy vein in the bend of my arm.
I lanced them both with flowers from another
country. You should have seen it.

Years of that until the windows were full
of a juice called methadone designed I guess
to sweep the streets of me. I weighed myself down
with coats of it. I unplugged the voices of my friends.
The world? Fuck. I can't get enough of it.

Austin Hummell : ALIEN ABDUCTION

It must be a rupture like waking,
all that light, telepathy and dental work,
and like the sever in the sylvan groove
that secrets bad sex and calculus
you bury it, deeper than infancy,
deeper even than the memoir
closed by birth, each leaf a little mattress
beneath which the memory sits
like a shelled and irksome legume
not even the fussiest princess senses.

But in the face of every fetus
is an alien: the disproportionate
head, blunted and sexless, eyes
like raindrops, sleepy and dark.

If it was flesh that muffled the sound
of your mother's voice,
you might swear all talk was telepathy.
If born into a hospital fluorescence,
you might recall a blinding light,
what Saul saw and called God.

Or say your head pushed out ahead
of your shrunken and colored self,
the pressure it suffers might seem
a vice for curious surgery. Torn

from the warm swamp of her womb
against your living will, you'd remember
a struggle, like abduction, a gallery
of eyes and the naked sensation
of being watched, for the first time.

Austin Hummell : THE DESERTION OF NOUNS

First to go are the names of fruit
and the people you haven't loved.
The dental assistant who pats your shoulder
when the drill stops, the waitress whose smile
was broken by stroke, the mailman
with his tattoos and tramp of snow
in the late morning. Call him Karl,
Karl who you've seen in the produce aisle
talking to himself because he can't remember
if it's turnip or mustard greens
that the man he has loved for twenty one years
wants, the man he talks about on your porch
with uninterruptible speed but whose name
escapes you now like his illness, though you
recall its manifestation in spots,
in the gentling of memory. Spots
like the ones blooming beneath the tan
on your hands that you notice when
you take your uncle his omelet. For him
there is nothing so lucid as 10 am,
when the spills of breakfast settle
and a nephew returns with a tray of nouns
and a name just below his forehead.
Starts with a B. Even in the snarl of tissue
we call his brain you count one hundred
trillion synapses down which chemicals
still whip fibers and tear across cell divides—
one hundred trillion to lay down the jumpy tracks
of memory, nudge his blood, chill
what is left of terror, schedule sleep,
help him walk or shape a plan

to kill himself. *Bird*, he says, *Ethel Merman, with rope. The day I rubbed my friends from the Memorial Wall. Pomegranate.*

Melanie Jordan : I ENTER THE WORLD IN EVERY NAMEABLE WAY

I.

Eyes casting about for a stray hair you
might have shed, I pretend to dust
my furniture, my books, lightly
touching everything I say I own
because I cannot lay hands
on a single lash of yours today,
not even your soft curse as you blow out
a match. Evolved to a brain
larger than my ancestors', I do have
the capacity to want what I cannot see:
the figure casting shadow fingers on my wall,
a better bicycle, a ham sandwich.ABSTRACTIONS
paste themselves to my mental bulletin board
from a dictionary, though
the definition of *want* encompasses
a sand-flayed whale
on a shore I've never seen
in addition to the following:

>   When I was seven, my father's friend
>   died suddenly on the table
>   during eye surgery. He taught me
>   how to tell time though
>   he was nearly blind.
>   He smiled to hear me read.
>   I knew nothing
>   until Monday morning—
>   our car never slowed
>   at his usual waiting spot.

Sometimes when I read a clockface,
Ben's old-man coffee denim smell
and hat with the homemade band
float back abstract as 2:13 or 5:11.
Furthermore, the mules in harness
rotate the wheel, make molasses
as they did when I was a kid watching
from the grass with the old man.
When I hear Willie Nelson sing,
I think *time time time* because Ben's voice
sounded like his. Country songs
stand for those passengerless years.
Time is a personal abstraction.
I declare there are no abstractions
so long as a carpool is a void,
so long as a heart attack is a table
and heartbreak is a study lamp
burning into the advancing morning.
So long as failure is a hiking boot
with a hole.
An hour goes by with or without someone.
Time again called something else.
I dial the phone with my thumb
and hear it ring on your end
where you've been writing checks
all morning for bills, where you've
fanned out the stubs that stand
for your work. Before you answer,
you smoothe the signature line of ink
yoking you to your work, and when you pick up,
I ask you *Say your name. I want you
to say your name.*

II.

Seven million years ago at least
she stood upright and wished
an arc into the basin of her world
that made a scrap of bone a token.
Soon a petal became the dead.
Through her, fire became a hope.
Did hope ripple all the way
to George Berkeley, his notion that sense
and reason are the only doors to the world?
Three hundred years later we applaud
Woody Allen who says *it's hard …*
to get your heart and head together.
The punchline: in my case,
they aren't even friendly.
No more the false dichotomy, the stretch
like an infinite barbell weighted
on each end. In the space between voices
a single body reconciles.
Like Helen Keller at the well,
with the word *water* burning cold
on her waking hand.
Your name is lavender and a brown dog.
I've come to hold your name
like a duck's bill scoops a pond.
All you've taken in and my third eye,
a smoke ring broken on its own composure,
a yellow bloom in the dust,
a white-footed mouse, shrapnel, the night
we said we will not leave this garden
until everything is named.
I enter the world in every way.
Your name: the Sunday
you were born, the first current of air
that passed over your body.

Melanie Jordan : ORNITHOLOGIST'S SUITE

Before night ends, before my wild alarm,
black shoulders and diamond-chip eyes: I
bolt upright at the figure near my bed, but

blue mercy seeps into the room as dawn,
bare and watered-down in gray rain, brings
birds with names I don't know for all the world,

birds so calm the day may have gone deaf.
Before long, it's plain I forgot to set the clock.
Barely any light squeaks through my clear window.

Black wings, black beaks in pantomime,
blue silk the only sound as I tie my robe, its
bolt of cloth seemingly bigger than the world, its

bolt of cloth like a cold damping mist, printed with
birds and cherry trees: indigo buntings, jays
blue and depicted perfectly, as though alive. Once

before, I woke up backwards, completely startled
black-tempered, dream-governed, the cogs and springs
bare in my head, churning overtime so I could hardly

bear the residue of my own thoughts, their carnivale
bolted with wings and worms, with the crying maw,
black gullet the first thing a nestling knows.

Birds that are half machine, like something from Bosch
before Bosch ever put brush to canvas, before he
blew shavings from his work desk and began to sketch

blue earth transparent as a bubble,
bare of humans or animals, the primordial state
before any kind of entropic garden emerged

bolted through with our supposed bodily sins.
Birds with beaks made monstrous by art,
black honey on their bills where they've probed

black hearts. Over me, my father stood
blue in the pane-light, watching me sleep, his
birds no comfort to me or him because my life,
barely held together with will and fatigue,
bolted together by a broken marriage, fitfully slept
before him, and he hadn't seen this woman before,

barely twenty-six with withered wings, having
bolted when her house went up in blue smoke.
Before, he saw his black-eyed girl, intact.

Melanie Jordan : ELEGY FOR OPRYLAND

Coasting, I resented my bike's brakes, hated
caring about an end to motion and to the wind
carving my spoke-gaps. My brother was gone
caving and camping where I could not go,
calling over his shoulder—always the kiddie
carousel for me, the swingset, etc., but that

carousel, the one my father and I rode each summer
coasted, lurched, broke full down, recovered. We
recalled no time it had been fluid. We'd heard:
carefully it had been exhumed from some desert
cave, someone had opened numbered boxes to find
carved cherubs, velvet carriages in pieces, horses

carved so realistically as to foam at the bit, their
carousel a parade of divans, baroque
cavernous cars wracked with the sound of gears
coasting, or trying to. In these coaches we were
carried over and over, summer after summer,
calling to us, my mother, *the park's closing*,

calling to us, calliope, the mouths of the painted
carved bodiless cherubim. As a teenager, I didn't
care when the park removed the old German
carousel and replaced it with another, a polished
coasting design: tigers, ostriches, bears freed from their
caves. Years later the amusement park

caved to the pressure of capitalism; a conference
call settled it, and Opryland shut down gradually,
coasting to a halt, became a shopping mall

carved from the ruins of roller coasters, the new
carousel, an arcade and acres of track that had
carried water and wheels, screaming hundreds

carried on finite journeys, uphill, down, through
caves constructed of concrete, endlessly
carouseled in pursuit of fun, whatever people
call fun at least, each roller coaster an attempt to
carve fun from fright, to hurt, to ultimately
coast into the station scared and laughing,

carried to safety, usually, as you call out:
cavernous lungs, your carving hoarse voice—
roller coaster, carousel, rusting in an open field.

Melanie Jordan : INVOCATION TO THE GOD OF X

Xeric: adjective for desert, or anything sucked dry and coping with x number of droplets evaporated or stolen, evacuated like Athens as Xerxes burned the Acropolis temples. Even the Parthenon, extant war-goddess temple, razed in its original form, enemies xenon-like in their permeation, there before anyone knew, troops like xerox copies of themselves swarming sacred ground. But not

xerox copies, because each was each, like Shi Huang Di's xeric terracotta warriors, their thousand expressions unique like xenon, the odorless, colorless element useful in its rarity. To its x-axis, razed, the first Parthenon, because King Xerxes dreamed: extant, a tall stranger ghost-oracle, howling havoc.
Xerxes sweating terror, recanting reluctance for war.

Xerxes, even in his arrogance, had the good sense to fear, and I xeroxing handouts for my students with the US at war, know no extant love in the young for Herodotus, as though his history, xeric and crotchety, cannot possibly trouble the present of Generation X, or Y, or whatever sub-final character we're calling them.
Xenon desk lamps burn black noise along the halls.

Xenon: Greek, means *stranger*. I am a stranger in these halls as Xerxes in fallen dust of years is, his native name, Khashayar Shah x'ed out in favor of the Greek name, a tyranny of history repeated, xeroxed sheets by the ream informed by a name removed from its source, xeric bone bleaching away from its watery host of blood and muscle, extant name out of water like a dry pump without oil.

Extant, extant. It still means here, I say. They don't have dictionaries.
Xenon was here before we knew it was, discovered 1898.
Xeric, remember? We talked about that word once before.

Xerxes the Persian King, assassinated around four-six-five BCE.
Xeroxed copies of the essay are coming down the rows.
X as in Malcolm, as in Roman numeral, as in wrong answer, try again.

X-rays of human suspicion, imagine, would yield a black puddle
extant and growl-inducing as a bone in a yard full of hounds.
Xeroxed flyers cover the walls, conflating terror with faith,
xenophobia in neon, nearly, and a colleague begs me to help pull them down.
Xerxes awaits, I tell him, I can't just now, my class, my
xeric heart shriveling as I turn, his hands full of crumpled paper.

Xenon lamps scour seabeds; if only they could see my expatriate heart.
Khashayar Shah, foolish king, no one has learned from you, extant only
xeric tomb like a great terracotta vase. Time and greed. Xerox, xerox.

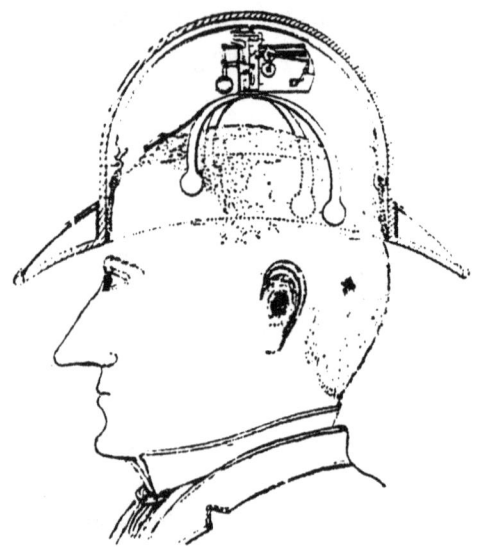

A Mechanical Hat Tipper.

When the wearer meets a lady an automatic mechanism lifts the hat.

Melanie Kenny : PARLOR

Blue ink. Blue heart. A way to start in deep
as dye through a vessel tints lymph's branched trail.
Cut cells, glass slides. The needle pricks skin's veil.
I forget my girl days of curls and pleats.
My shoulder brushed the door jamb and clay bells
ring out reproof. If only I could stand,
my mouth would say: sugar, I'm your dark ant.
I drank it all, no ice. Red, black label.
Decisions should be made any way but this:
train wreck ahead, jumped tracks, the engineer
amazed he's not the one dead. You're too near.
You think I should let them. A few quick tests.
I want what I'm afraid they'll give a name:
murmuring valve through which this hard need came.

C. F. Kimball : WINTERKILL GUEST BOOK

Busted pocket warmer. Drawer of owl pellets
In vials divorced from labels. Rod and fly,
Rod and fly across the wainscot. Taut belly
Of a German urn. Railroad ties—unaccountably.

—

The curtains only move one way, sucked to cup
Like sailcloth against the rotted screens all night.
Where were you? Tonguing snow banks, so you dreamed,
Snow hares bottoms-up inside their warrens.

—

Burned a cache of clippings as the need arose,
The bulk from *True Crime* and Diderot's *Encyclopedia*.
I would like to ply my trade in knee pants
And a dusted wig. I would like a solid alibi.

—

Days of pinhole cameras. As you tracked the weak
Spots in the ice, my own vessel took a vole
Skull breached by taper-flame. In its sockets,
I would find another phylum's skulking fugitive.

—

It was safe to shoe across the bay
To visit Ollie's monument. *One-Man Injun
Band—Barkeep, Father—Bless the Goner—*
Can't brook old facts: Our Ollie an invention.

—

Sussed out by neighbors, would we flee their greeting.
All signs point to yes, and yet you bang out
"Gypsy Rover" on the upright like Mr. Oliver
LaFourge himself, friend to man and water spirit.

—

Pantry survey for a pair of starving hobos:
Apples, sauced, apples, peeled and whole, rhubarb
Stew, Eisenhower-era. Stew, Reagan-era,
Carter beets, supper beans, Sunday-dinner beans.

—

The mantel fawns in pert communion—
Sipping, prancing, womb-glaze ever glinting.
Oh fever Christmas! Oh God we have met
And never known. Play that song again. Again.

—

Not dead, only sleeping where October left them,
Where you figure-eight in shadow. Not dead.
Trudging leather-shod through litanies of minerals,
My blood goes uneclipsed. King of chapped lips.

—

Evenings of Canasta by the oil lamp
In this marsh of dust and mangy pelts, and you.
But days! The sun pierces sooner. Trestle music
In the distance. The sky's dome pried loose.

—

I read the Knights of Pythias, in idea-form,
Descended from a rope of cloud to scout this broad
Peninsula. As if exile coaxed a civil grace
From men by means of schoolroom rites and self-regard.

—

You heard it, too: a ripsaw's burr across the road.
A paddle stabbing ice. Lone church bell from the point,
Cold as the palm that tugged it. And the lore of derby
Season on the radio. Tonight, you heard it too.

—

Home from a trek, and handprints black the entryway.
Aborted ransack, or Ollie wants the light to flood
The drawers, to stir the ashes with his shallow breath.
Pack your case tonight. Sojourn overturned.

—

Though we have spared the rarest volumes from the stove,
And every barren season wants for testimony…
All the same, there's no recompense for jam and spirits;
Their vessels cram the shed. We are not much for stewardship.

—

To every rotten stump a hole for light, for curled
Parasites the wind would scotch . To every teeming thaw
A chorus of flues and ores. To every ferrous shore
A wall of shanty-smoke the branches will disperse.

Matthew Kirby : THE SNOW GOOSE, A DOSSIER

Reign, Characteristics of:

The snow goose's reign was characterized by blood.
The official emblem of the snow goose's blood reign was the image of the elegantly curved neck of the snow goose itself.
The adjective most frequently employed by the people to describe the neck of the snow goose was "perilous."
The snow goose exploited the people remorselessly.
The people made quilts with pictures of sea animals on them.
The quilts were a tradition of sorts in the lands controlled by the snow goose.
The people, however, no longer made the quilts using traditional means.

Common Eccentricities:

It was not uncommon for the snow goose to become furiously bored with the situation it had created.
It was not uncommon for the snow goose to stalk the streets of the lands it controlled, its perilous neck flashing white as it struck the life-blood from people of the land.
It was not uncommon for the snow goose to pluck whole shipments of newly constructed quilts from the docks and hurl them over the lip of the volcano.
It was not uncommon for the people who worked the docks from which the quilts were exported to get goose bumps upon sighting the perilous neck-flag of their savage ruler, the snow goose.
It was not uncommon, despite its frequent savagery and indiscretion, for the snow goose to receive tribute from foreign dignitaries.
It was not uncommon for foreign dignitaries, lured by sandy

beaches and a thriving quilt-making culture, to make frequent voyages to the lands controlled by the snow goose.

It was not uncommon for the snow goose to host lavish dinner parties, attended by foreign dignitaries, at which feasting and reveling were the dominant modes of behavior.

Lands, Outstanding Geographic features of:

The volcano was a major landmark.

The lands controlled by the snow goose did not have any other outstanding geographic features so the volcano would have to suffice.

The volcano had been dormant for a long period of time but sometimes it sputtered.

The snow goose once tried to tell some foreign dignitaries at a dinner party that the reason the volcano sometimes sputtered was that it sometimes grew hungry and that the reason the snow goose sometimes hurled the quilts over the lip of the volcano was to appease the volcano and that, ultimately, the reason the volcano remained dormant was that the snow goose appeased it with the blankets.

The foreign dignitaries knew better than to follow this remark with any of their own remarks.

The night air swallowed up their indiscreet discretion.

The avenue or "leak" through which the people heard about the snow goose's remark was the porter's protege, who the snow goose would have surely slain if he hadn't believed him to be utterly deaf.

Generalizations Better Left Unmade:

No one can claim to know the whole story of the snow goose and the lands it controlled.

None of the borders of those lands continue to maintain the shape the snow goose had originally given them.
Not that anybody has ever heeded those borders anyway.
Never were there borders more flagrantly flouted than those borders.
Not in recent memory were there border-flouters of such dubious character and transparent purpose.
Nary a one of them, when apprehended, expressed the slightest degree of regret concerning their egregious misdeeds.
Nil, in the end, was the number of those blackguards spared punishment at the hands of the snow goose.

Recent Developments:

As of late, the snow goose is rumored to be hiding in a lean-to constructed of car doors in Birmingham.
As of late, the snow goose is rumored to be a broken old creature, filled to brim with regret for the blood that once characterized its reign
As of late, the snow goose is rumored to have taken up fishing, a sport at which it is rumored to be extremely unlucky.
The snow goose has seven grandchildren: Jen, the rain goose; Baba, the mist goose; Glen, the bluster goose; Todd, the goose of the north; Bing, the desert goose; Hershel, the grey goose and Emily—the only one rumored to have inherited the snow goose's perilous and lovely neck—the ice goose.
Emily, perilous Emily: She is the one the people are murmuring about.
Emily, fair Emily: Let not your birthright be your fate!
As of late, the snow goose is rumored to have been seen whistling, strutting about tunefully before its hut made of car doors in Birmingham, waiting for the late winter frosts to come and carry off its soul.

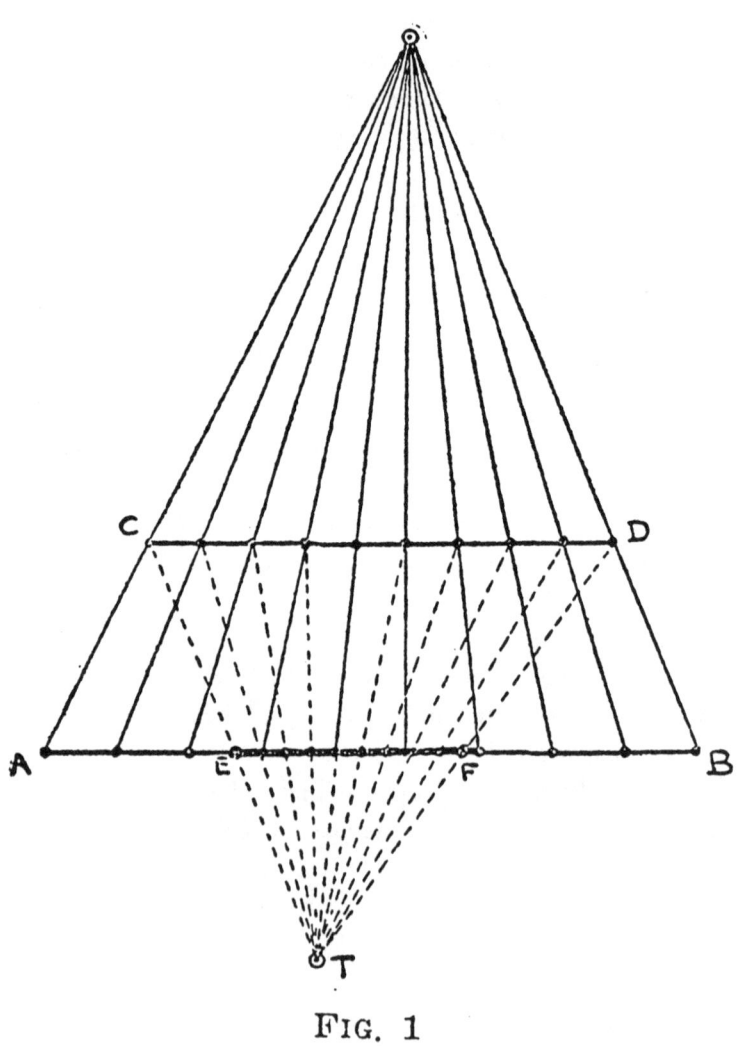

Fig. 1

L. S. Klatt : AFIELD

Something old to fondle, Osage
fruits, the stooping

transplants—my brother & I threw 'em
I-275
eastbound oranges, sky chopper traffic

Semis kicked hedge-apples interstate
into fences where the sycamores

slough their skins, the retro-
grade bluegrass
stored in Mason

& the milky planets
Bisquick & *Kellogg's* variety packs

such green children
sweet blister corn, reentry

L. S. Klatt : WANDERING OF LIGHT

You graze me, purple star
sad blood sack
you dead End

Nebula

plastic-bag-pinched
I drop you in a can
oblate

look up at heedless
the headlights half-decimate

moon, Jupiter

I was sad when the Hyphen
said unto me
go up into the House

of the Interpreter

Sharon Kraus : GHOST

bye bye smoke
    spoken to the lifting, watered
        air from the spout the
       gone sabbath wick
      I've said,
  Is there any such thing?
    but/therefore his interest in ghosts :
    wisp   drift
    (water that is not
   itself, though you are
   told otherwise). Only the
   sufferer can see one, for example;
    only the still-suffering dead can make
    such noise. [He cannot bear watching
    me hold another baby, despite repeated
    exposures. The child wants to take in (soak
;   )all care] babychildbaby   wordscrywords
   Wishing to speak to a someone now   absent
   : a holding of mere air   For solace I ask of
   the person I birthed (he is drawn to that which
   frightens and to that which cowersyetspeaks)
   He prefers making his own stories now; once
  uponatime there was a Mommy, a Daddy, a
  child, and a not-nice Ghost   who ate people!
Another parent accepting death in wartime An-
other found breathing beneath rubble, on the
sixth day. The husband spills seed on her belly.
The cut-glass sphere breaks open the light. Rain-
bows -volving on the walls. Things existing
Not existing. Wished-for. Despite.

Corinne Lee : PAST + PAUCITY + H_2O

Numbering the willow's leaves,
not these pages. As solace.
Because anyone can read
the entire history
of collision
in our picture. Our last
sea-sand-mud bath, a digging morning,
plump pails, hopscotching
home on stones
that could be true.
At dusk, mussels exploding
from the pot.
Behind every real object,
there is an object
dreamed.
An ambiguous bile color
can pull me back
to that time.
The children bedwetting,
your phobia re stray
parings. Skinflint
embraces. One rule
of the waters:
When a crest
and trough converge,
they cancel each other
into a plane.
Which were you? And I was—?

Matthew Lippman : AND EVERYWHERE IT'S FLORIDA

What I did, I lied.
I lied about the Cremora Food Truck hijacked,
brought to Boston, blown up,
just to get all that white powder up in the air,
just to get all the kids to listen;

I lied about the money and the hungry zookeeper
who killed two giraffes with a bullhorn then wheeled out the
Hibachi.

I lied about living rooms on fire
and dead cowboys on my lawn
who rode clean out of thin air
before I shot 'em with my six shooter,
cried *Geronimo*,
broke down in hives
and got lost in the Hollywood tumbleweed.
All my life it's been helicopter blades in my spine;
all my life I've lied.

When I was six I didn't believe there were frogs in the pond
and lied that there were,
green ones with red tongues,
ones with the poisonous venom,
that they might bite me in the butt,
turn me into a ragged prince.

At fifteen I lied about my hair,
that is was short and clean
and that I was headed for the Marines,

become a three star general
then kick some serious ass in places I didn't even know existed,

like Tahoe,

go to Tahoe and mow the bastards down
in their ski-boot delirium,
their bunny-suit pirouette.

What I did,
I lied about hearing voices and nailing myself to a cross;
I lied about the visiting team and about the French Revolution,
that it happened on Suez soil
and that we live for love then die alone.

Maybe I didn't lie about that,
maybe that's all there is when the hotcakes come, a slab of butter,
a busty waitress named Charlene with the short skirt and large lips
and everywhere it's Florida.

I've been there once, I can't tell a lie,
to visit my grandmother,
then she died,
I didn't go to the funeral, what I did,
I stayed home and watched t.v.

Duane Locke : THE LOST CARNATION

The hole in the lapel now had only a stem,
A carnation stem.
The carnation believed in, lived by the categorical imperative.

The carnation went to assemblies and slept.
The carnation wanted to wear a hood,
But the request was denied.

The carnation admired the red fringe
On the tips of its ruffled petals.
No one ever noticed the red.

No one ever noticed the white.
No one ever noticed the ruffles.
The carnation stop believing the categorical imperative.

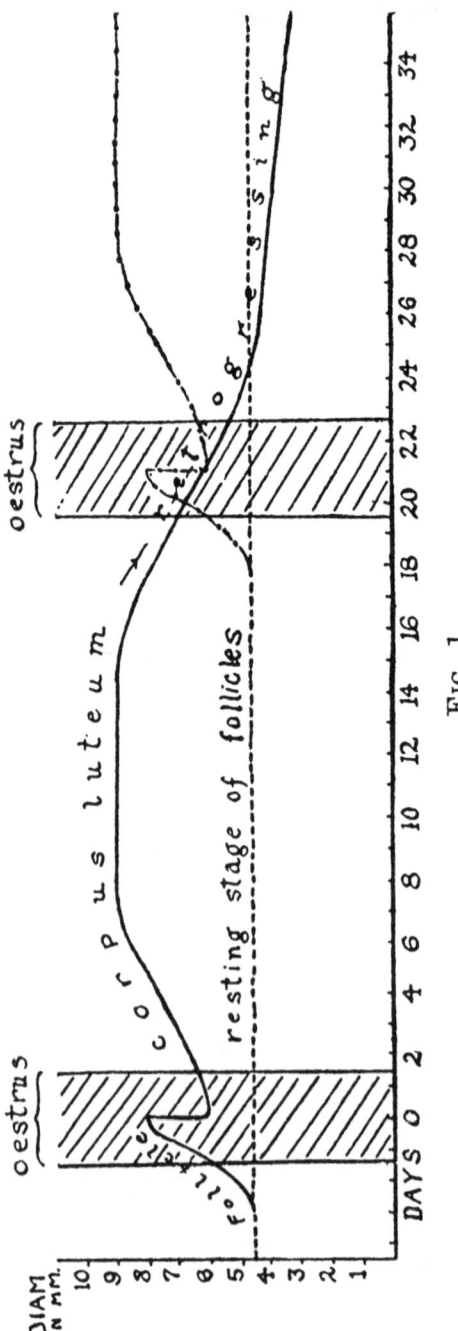

Fig. 1.

Diagram representing the ovarian cycle of the nonpregnant sow.

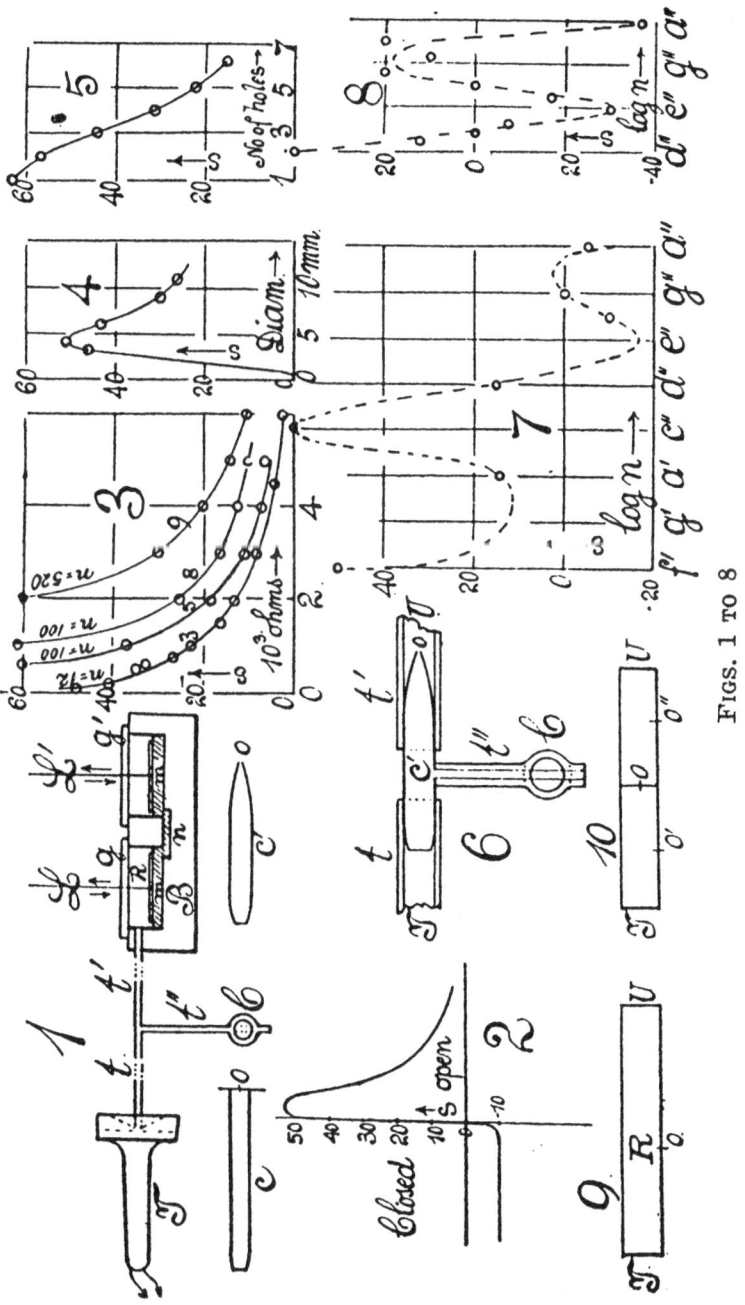

Figs. 1 to 8

Daniel Mahoney : TOILET FILL VALVE

Toilet remained "on" the whole night keeping
Sheila awake. This was not helped by the fact
that it was raining and the gutters were full of butternuts.
I slept through the night.

Removed the top of toilet and discovered
two bricks and a broken fill valve. (Sheila
uses bricks to save on the cost of water)
Fill valve filled toilet but continued to fill after full.

This is a problem.

(Joe Koch says toilets leak enough water
to fill an outdoor swimming pool such
as the one he and Wanda are planning to install.)

Used channel locks to remove fill valve and
brought the entire mechanism to Carr
for replacement.

Replacement box includes "shank washer",
"locknut", "cone washer" and "coupling nut". This
makes job easier than if box were empty.
Remember this next time.

Adjusted valve height to 11 inches which should
be high enough to save water in tank.

BRICKS ARE UNNECESSARY.

                    John
                    1/27/66

Daniel Mahoney : RADIAL SAW AND DADO BLADES

Bought new DADO SETS from Sears as they sent notice of a sale to the paper. This should make groove fitting all the more easy and allow corner joints to be flush no matter how big the frame.

Follow the illustrations on the box when attaching blades to this mechanism. Look at the cuts before attempting anything. This is not like Bob Petrin's jig saw.

(Call Bob Petrin about giving back his jig saw)

Mount the blade on arbor so that you can hand turn the blade backward. The teeth get set by tapping striker pin with a light hammer such as the small ball peen that is upstairs or in the pantry.

Featured cuts: "corner lap", "cross lap", "straight lap", "tee", "half lap miter", "miter box corner", "half gain", "rabbet", "notch".

When unsure about anything refer to the HANDBOOK OF CIRCULAR SAW BLADES AND POWER TOOL ACCESSORIES that is tacked to the jar board hanging above the workbench.

ALWAYS WEAR GLASSES.

        John
        5/10/66

Daniel Mahoney : SCARLET TANAGER

Placed the bird on the worktable under newspaper.
Packed beak and anus with padding to avoid
a mess. Made an anchor for the wings
with chains and fishhooks.

Cut and lifted up the skin as far as the beak.
Cut neck at the base of the skull, removed
brain, tongue, palate from occipital hole.

(Note that this needs to be done quickly
as skin may dry)

Made body form from wet straw and galvanized
wire. (a number 16 or 18 wire works well for this)
Inserted and filled every empty space inside
with padding.

Wrapped well in order to prepare for drying.
Note that this process can take several weeks.

Opened the mouth and puffed up the throat
with small pieces of wadding until it
was filled enough to be singing.

Eyelids raised with needle and thread so the eyes
will always show.

KEEP BIRDS AWAY FROM THE SUN.

                        John
                        2/14/79

Barbara Maloutas : PRACTICE 2

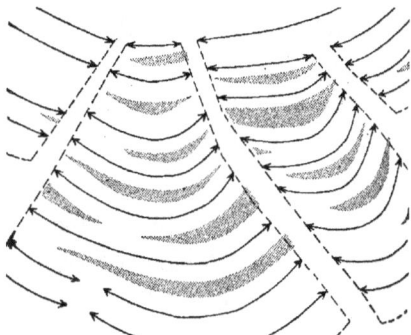

When everything has been said, I think we'll be quiet. We are actually afraid of what hasn't been said. Finally to arrive at quiet. If every word is said in every combination of words, where will we be and where. If one folds a paper fifty times in half, we will be half way to the sun. Even this is not enough for every word in every possible order.

Peter Markus : THE MOON IS A LIGHTHOUSE: REVISITED

Night after night after night after night we go, us brothers do, and look for the moon. Some nights the moon, even if the both of us brothers were boys born blind, we could feel it shining with our hands. On other nights, nights when the white of the moon is a lighthouse light no eyes or hands could see it in its whereabouts hiding, even on those nights, though, we know it is out there, in the dark, darkly shining, because we, us brothers, us boys, we can hear it sing. When the moon sings, us brothers, to the moon's crooning, we sit up in bed, we slip out of bed, and with our hands cupped round our ears we try to €nd where the moon is sleeping, figure out where it is hammocked between two stars. And on nights when the moon, it is cut in half, nights when it is half a brother, us brothers, one of us, we will go back inside into our own place of hiding, this, we figure, so that the moon won't feel so unwhole. And what about those other nights, those nights when the moon, it is a slipper made of ice, or glass, or star light? On nights such as those, we go and we get Girl and then we tell Girl to slip her muddy foot into the moon. When Girl slips her muddy foot into the moon, every time, the moon, with Girl's foot in it, it is a perfect fit. So then we sit back and watch Girl tip toe and tap dance the moon across the night time's sky, dancing until the sun sits up and begins to clap its hands, it stands up with its clapping, until this clapping turns to light.

Peter Markus : THE MOON IS A MOUTH, A BANJO, A DRUM

In the bunk bed that is above my head, Brother leans with his head over the edge to ask me, Brother, what is that sound? Us brothers, often at night, we hear sounds that brothers other than us, they do not hear them. Oh but this, this sound, there is no not hearing this sound. This sound, it is a song that is better than singing. This sound, the sound of it—its voice—it is coming not just from some body's mouth. This sound, it is coming from someplace else where the mouth that is making this sound—it is just one hole on that body. Outside our room, the moon, it is a hole in the sky where a light is pouring through. Us brothers, here in this light for us boys to look up at the sky by, we are standing up tall and tippy toe high so we are looking eye to eye with the moon. The moon, Brother tells me this, looks like a banjo. So Brother's eye sees this like this. Brother makes with his mouth that sound that a banjo makes when a banjo's being fingerpicked by a hand that knows just what it is doing. The moon, tonight, banjo bellied, it is so big and it is so white that its bigness is bigger than the sky that is behind it—that black night mud that holds the moon up in all of its light. Tonight, this moon: it's not a banjo the way that Brother says he sees it. No, the moon, tonight: this moon is a wide open mouth that, in this brother's eyes, this moon has swallowed up the rest of its body. And so what we do, look at us brothers as we do this doing, we reach up with our muddy boy hands to push this light back into this moon's mouthy hole. But the moon, to us brothers too, the moon in all of its whiteness, it swallows us brothers up inside. Inside, there is this light here on the inside of this place. In this light, us brothers, we see that the moon, it is not a banjo. The moon, it is a drum. And us brothers, here inside, down in this hollowed out space, we are the sound that the moon sometimes makes when we pound, when we hammer, when we nail, when we bang: we hit, and hit, our muddy fists up against it.

Clay Matthews : NANCY REAGAN DRAG

Three in the morning, because my wife's asleep
and it's come to this. After two days of searching
for Nancy Reagan's voice, I'm in pantyhose,
a magenta skirt, a rubber Nancy mask I found
at an antique store for three dollars. And it's hell
being the first lady—my leg hairs pulled through
an unnaturally orange shade of flesh, trying to breath
behind this mask with the earrings that look
like they weigh three pounds each. I'm suffocating,
but learning, how to save my air for the right words,
how to appear a symbol of strength and wife
in a collar that closes around my neck like a choke-chain.
And I've found something here—a way to address Ronald,
that magical bean, all wrinkles and unwavering chuckle:
My dear and loving husband, let me count the ways.
How I've saved you on stage, whispered the answer
in that enormous, pliable lobe of an ear. And your staff
laughing and talking behind our backs, you the idiot, I
the dragon lady. Let them talk. Let them laugh.
Let them call me crazy for consulting the astrologer
after you were shot, the meeting the three of us had
together, the one she and I had alone, that I didn't tell
you about, couldn't, Oh Ronald, I had to know
what would become of the lady when her fool
of a king was gone. Where did I lose that something,
our young love we found shooting *Hellcats of the Navy*,
gone somewhere between red ribbons. Just say no.
It's enough to make a girl lonely, to cross her legs
even when they fall asleep, waiting for the day
it all falls apart, like some terribly expensive
China collection, broken piece by piece.

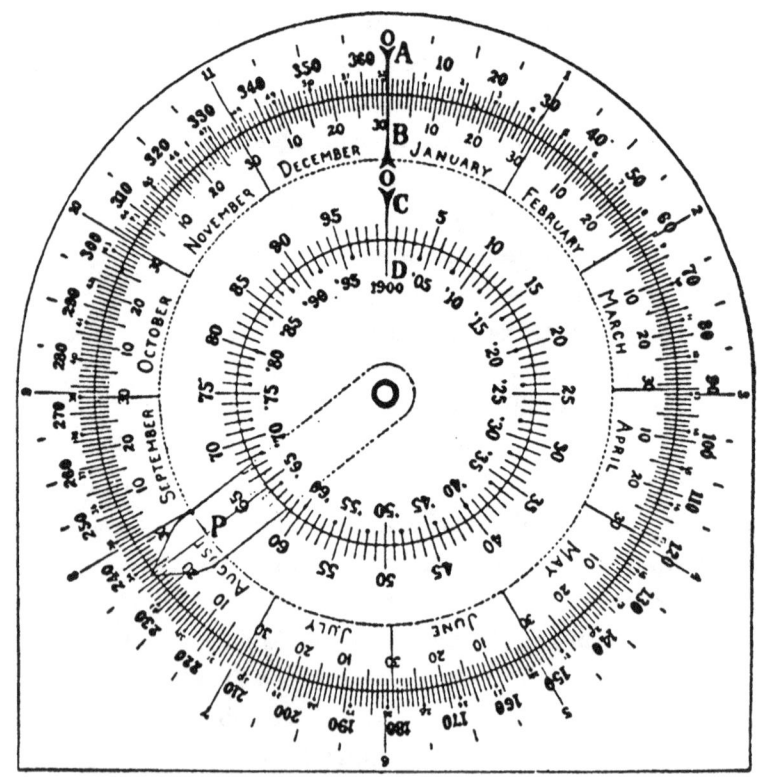

Age-Computing Circular Slide Rule

Deirdra McAfee : ABSENCE ARTIST

In 1928 I washed up, wet and fatherless, in Union Beach, New Jersey, delivered from my mother Mary to wear my father's name: Nathwell Tate. Nat Tate I went by, Nat Tate I signed my work, name and work now lost as waterlogged Atlantis. They never found my body. Full fathom five thy father lies.

My father was and he wasn't. A cipher, a story. I was four when he died. Or I died before him. Or he died or didn't die before I was born. They never found my body. I never found his body. He knew my mother but not me. He came, he went. A version, a void, a grave. She said he was a Nantucket fisherman. Sometimes. She said he drowned before me. Full fathom five.

Lies that came and went. Wet dreams of death and drowning. My father was a naval architect. Submariner. Deep-sea diver. Merchant seaman. Missing. Killed in action. Dead in the water. Those are pearls that were his eyes. Sleepless as the river, unburied in a watery grave, locked in Davy Jones's locker.

He came, he went. They never found our bodies. A cipher, a story. My mother Mary had a talent for polishing glassware. A barmaid, maybe, whom a sailor pressed up against, pressed in upon. He came, he went. A version, a void. Floating me, beaching me, drowning. Full fathom five. A grave.

Or the darker version, wherein he pays for his pleasure, a shadowy urgent dockside encounter. I've had a few myself. *Under thy shadow by the piers I waited*, wrote my other father, the one who died when I was four. The father I adopted, not the one adopting me. Hart Crane, my chosen father, friend, beloved. Who died when I did, at thirty-two. A shadow, a darkness. *Sleepless as the river*. He died and didn't die; he lives in words. But all of us are dead now. Null, void, grave. They never found our bodies.

My mother, born Mary Tager, became the widow Mary Tate. Self-inventor, shape-changer, tale-teller; serving-girl, glass-washer. Kitchen maid, then cook, at Windrose, a small elegant estate on the wrong side of Peconic Bay. A sea-change erased me, perhaps: nothing earlier remains, no place or face, scent, sight, or sound precedes Windrose. I was three and lived with her there, "below the bridge," the locals say, north among potato fields and fishing-boats instead of south in the fancy Hamptons.

She died before me. I was eight. One icy morning in Riverhead, Long Island, a delivery van delivered her from life into dead and bloody nothingness, broke her bones. River and island, full fathom five. When someone interrupted schoolyard softball to say so, I thought he was joking.

A departure I wasn't witness to, a void unavoided. Thus I was delivered from her a second time, February 1936. *Already snow submerges an iron year*, wrote my other father, a lover of boys like me. He wrote that six years before she died. Two years before he drowned. We never met. I never found his body.

> *Often beneath the wave, wide from this ledge*
> *The dice of drowned men's bones he saw . . .*

The dice of her thrown bones delivered me up to her employers, the Barkasians, for adoption. Luck, it looked like. Money. Clever Peter could afford to ignore the Great Depression; he sold Albany Paper to DuPont for cash in 1927 and retired rich at 36. For childless Irina, his wife, marriage was the great depression.

Peter fell in love with his new son, said a woman years later, my art dealer, who was maybe one of my lovers herself. Was she? Who were my lovers? Variety and brief encounters. They came, they went, and I did, too. Lost, obliterated, even to me, when I walked underwater and vanished.

Fell in love with me, what did that mean? I was the emptiness Peter meant to fill, the story he meant to finish. He found my body, kept it, but I reclaimed it later. And still later he never found my body. They never found my body. He found my talent and fed it and tried to buy all my drawings and paintings. Fitted out a pretty little studio in the garden, a gilded cage.

Later I made pictures he didn't like and sold them to others. Later still, practically too late, I took them back. Fire sank them. Full fathom five. So that rich Peter couldn't own me. I died before him, saw the dice of drowned men's bones.

—

Once the woman dealer found me, I left Windrose but not my allowance, moved to metropolis, fell in with bohemians, drank all night at the Cedar Tavern, half-heard endless slurred and smoky esthetic arguments, earthshaking to all but me. Fell through uncounted affairs, fragile women, seafaring men, strangers, acquaintances, distances. Worked hard, drank harder, said little, thought less.

I seemed to myself to be vanishing. Sober and standing beside my brilliant uproarious friends, I shrank. Rested and well-fed, athwart lithe lovers, I floated out of reach, though my willing skillfulness pleased them and they pleased me. Everything felt temporary; I was an outline of needs, wants, hungers.

Sweating and sated with sex, I burned to be drunk; drunk and disordered, I bolted sex or work or food; painting or drawing, I had to lock myself in, block my rush to empty out my afternoons in any easy hot bed or dark bar.

"Around 1950 everyone just got drunk and the whole art world went on a long, long bender," an artist's wife, a nobody like all the wives, said later. The wives cleaned up after and cried over the men, except the few wives who were artists, too, and outdrank and outdeceived them.

I lean and loafe at my ease, observing. With them but not of them. The New York School: bad drunks, ambitious seers having amazing visions. Having messy affairs, brawls, and drunken blackouts. Starring in fast red stories full of sudden death or anticlimactic strung-out dissolution.

Unlike them, I had success without ambition, free of struggle or setback. Peter monopolized my work and paid my dealer well, made me her best-seller. Starved me on false plenty, separated me from my scratching, striving colleagues, tamed my aims. Finally I made things Peter didn't want, and he loosened the leash. Although he couldn't drop it.

—

In September 1959, still trying to buy me, feed my talent, win me back, Peter purchased Europe. Georges Braque, old enough to be too old to be my father, entertained us in Normandy. Bourgeois paterfamilias, rock of reality, still reworking paintings at 78. Forged in art, tempered by faith and solitude. A presence.

He died after me but lives on, as I do not. "You can never be good enough," Braque's life and work said. Not his words, which were: Persevere; enlarge your gift. But I fled Peter and Europe because I suspected the truth.

I drank enough when I got back to work it out. Afloat on a flood-tide of booze, afire with its fumes, I understood at last: "You can never be good enough to be immortal." I saw cold-eyed the paltry work, pitiful talent, stunted genius of Peter's pet. Saw single instead of the double way an artist has to see.

And saw the single solution, a double death, the easy sensible response to an extended invitation. "Leave a space," I said to myself, slurring the slippery words, "neither corpse nor corpus. A pyre, then a plunge. Vacancy, your fathers' tradition. Loss, the family legacy."

I told myself, or the liquor told me, that the writers and painters and hangers-on who bought my work and got blotto with me, blotted me and themselves out, they, too, would someday sink. Famous, or almost famous, somewhat known, or unknown, submerged in an iron year, some other year, some later year, they'd join me, jetsam irretrievable.

This was my chance to get there first, cleanse the record, sift the archive, clear my name. Still a promising artist, not yet a disappointing one. Still time to escape in time.

—

As my chosen father knew. In 1932, after his Guggenheim year in Mexico, a vain year, an iron year, unable to conquer his planned poem on the Spanish conquest, Hart Crane sailed home on the Orizaba. Voyaging from Vera Cruz, True Cross, with his paramour Peggy Cowley, he made a pass belowdecks. The sailor beat him up.

The bottom of the sea is cruel, Crane wrote in 1926, sailing already toward fame and his fate:

There is a line
You must not cross nor ever trust beyond it
Spry cordage of your bodies to caresses
Too lichen-faithful from too wide a breast.

He disobeyed himself and crossed. Travel teaches terrible things; voyagers shipwreck beyond the fatal line, explorers drown against the too-wide breast of their undertaking. Mexico for him. France for me. True Cross. Saw true and crossed.

Out of some subway, scuttle, cell or loft, a bedlamite speeds to thy parapets, he wrote in 1930 to the Brooklyn Bridge. *Tilting there, shrill shirt ballooning, a jest falls from the speechless caravan.* Two years later Crane, too, tilted. Not a bedlamite, a realist. Who crossed from the *Orizaba* into endless mortality, not good enough, a jest falls.

—

Crane's first book was *White Buildings*, the name I chose for my second series, cut short by my departure, another body never found. *The Bridge*, his second, was my first. "I like bridges," I told another nobody, Logan Mountstuart, failed writer and minutely attentive daily diarist. "So strong, so simple—but imagine what flows in the river underneath."

The city's discards, useless, used up, empty. Offal, garbage, disposable temporary anonymous unidentifiable trash. And beneath that, the jetsam, all that sinks, whatever isn't light enough to live or real enough to last. *The bottom of the sea is cruel,* Crane wrote.

But was it? When he reached it, did he find it so? There the open spaces, the empty stories, the varied versions of all my fathers, my only true lovers, waited to embrace me. Cold but not cruel, they mingled me into their indifference. Those are pearls that were our eyes. No more striving or failing, rising or falling, no more friends, enemies, lovers, ecstasy, pain. Our bodies were not found.

—

After I went to Europe, met Picasso, lunched with Braque, I

rushed to New York, afire to retract my work. "Here lies one whose name was writ in water," said Keats about himself. About me, too, more than half in love with easeful death. In December I persuaded the owners to return my pieces for reworking. In early January I stole Peter's trove at Windrose, years of sketches, drawings, paintings. Then I reworked every piece. In fire. Erased myself, unmade, undid, unbuilt.

I lit myself with liquor to help me burn away my work, burned my name just days before I walked the waves. Wrote my name on water, vanished my works and days, quenched name foretold drenched body.

I burned all the bridges I could find, more than 200. The drawings invited their fiery fate hungrily, cascades of bright ashes and sparks leaped into the sea-gray sky. The paintings gave hot oblivion a warmer welcome still, their colors ran into the flames, melting and changing, iridescent as they vanished.

The burning body of my work was mine to destroy; rich Peter would get no richer betting on me. The drowning body of my self was mine to sink, something else he couldn't own. Ashes to ashes, dust to dust, nothing to nothing, a lovely symmetry in that.

Finally I'd found my ambition, discovered my desire—the long longing to join my missing fathers in the void, become no more, *nauta*, sunken sailor, naught. Wash away the space I was—life, loves, work, talent—restore it to perfect nothingness. *Only in darkness is thy shadow clear.* Full fathom five, shining in the depths. Burnished and empty like you before me, O my fathers! Fire-scoured and pure.

—

That done, half a month into the iron year of 1960, my thirty-second year, I bought my ticket. In a breezy, bitter January sundown, as the shuddering Staten Island ferry steered for the dusk between Liberty and the Jersey shore, I shed hat, coat, and scarf and climbed over a guard-rail guarding nothing.

The wind I leaned into was biting, cold as the steely chords of the Brooklyn Bridge, the harp and altar of my chosen father. Passengers shouted, seabirds cried, a steamship somewhere groaned, but I heard only wind and the words I whispered as I waited to join my fathers, my brothers. *Under thy shadow by the piers I waited.* Twenty-eight years astern, I crossed Crane's line. I flew for the water, wings wide.

Crane saw the Brooklyn Bridge lift night in its arms. But his life was water under the bridge in the dark, like my father's and my own. Like them I drowned, disappeared. We all drowned. *Only in darkness is thy shadow clear.* Water and fire rush to fill space, fall or rise, wash out or burn off, clean and burnish. Leave no trace.

Silver-paced as though the sun took step of thee, beloved Brooklyn Bridge, you watched me board the boat and turn toward night. When the ferry faced Union Beach, I jumped. Like Crane, my lover, leader, chosen father.

I whispered his words as I waited and then went:

Again the traffic lights that skim thy swift
Unfractioned idiom, immaculate sigh of stars,
Beading thy path—condense eternity:
And we have seen night lifted in thine arms.
Under thy shadow by the piers I waited;
Only in darkness is thy shadow clear.
The City's fiery parcels all undone,
Already snow submerges an iron year...

As Nat Tate's son, I looked back to Union Beach. As Hart Crane's son, I jumped. Only in darkness is thy shadow clear. Mere flesh, instantly frigid, quickly breathless, lungs icy sodden sponges. No one found my body, submerged in an iron year, like my dead fathers Nathwell Tate and Hart Crane. Far down, full fathom five.

—

Three days later, since I'd failed to rise again, since poor Mary, my dead mother, had ceased relations with the sea and could deliver me no more, rich Peter and the rest packed up my studio downtown. My affairs were in perfect order: extinguished, scoured, bare.

A single new painting, fatherless, unfinished, stood calm in my swept vacant purified studio: *Orizaba/Return to Union Beach*. White winter light played across blues, purples, blacks, bold as bruises. When Mountstuart explained the title, Peter burst into tears, a father at last. Outside, snow submerged an iron year.

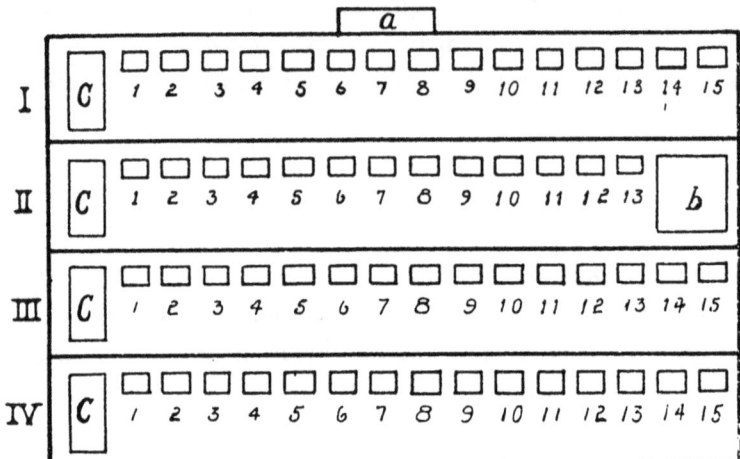

FIG. 8. Arrangement of a synoptic exhibit illustrating the history of sculpture as elaborated in the U. S. National Museum. *I.*, Series of tools and appliances. *II.*, Series of aboriginal American sculptures. *III.*, Series of oriental sculptures. *IV.*, Series of Mediterranean sculptures. *a*, Case label. *b*, General descriptive label. *cccc*, Series labels. 1, 2, 3, 4, etc., Specimen labels.

Jeffrey Morgan : HOW WORD IS PASSED

I wake to prime numbers written in blue ink on my forearms.
The television's sparkling reflection selling in the glaze
of her eyes the snow storm that will keep us.
How long have I been asleep?
I remember tendencies and sentiment of form:
"Words like pieces of topaz." Minutes/hours/days/years ago the glint
Of all of Eighth Street stocking up at Gristedes. Supple glare ringing off
White tile   shovel blades   excited teeth
Thinning to this deliberate process.
This is the shadow of the atomic bomb? Half-life moon. Seepage.
Sunlight coppering collar bones. My grandfather dropping
The star from our name: Morganstern. Orange gears of horizon.
When someone says: *the double meaning of morning.*
We've been told things and so we tell others.

Rachel Moritz : TUNING THE INSTRUMENT

1

Earliest erotic memory would be a woman's voice comb like on back

Spine is the wash

Odd fixation on checkered floor paneling makes memory a delicious sound pattern

Outside fabrics of other stories: hogs squeal across the bay Slaughter-housed, spotted junks and their families bob waves

And so the sea opens a hundred leagues around a girl's back, body piece electrifying as flash like wave or serpent

2

Would the piece after all function as an island?

Like in furious adolescence when all raged against those billboards treating woman like a hog or stud steer. Loin, hunk, ass, dinner!

Constellation of desired parts under which true
life is keeping

The canoe wants to hug the island's shore

No one departs or arrives
In winter it's only dry tree branch and unsnapped underbrush

This might be the other shore

3

For things, she troubles hungering

Summer sheet

And in the zap of midday some loose tree snapping

The snap itself not loud enough, more like a lilt or hook or a slight mouth gasp. She tries to snag herself, some part, foot, ankle, calf, anterior. Then she is going through the leaves on the end of a tree and feeling the wind through each piece

4

To inhabit perception of nonperception or of

Passivity

Body giant chunk or trunk

Inside the case, an elephant without tusks

5

Both equally difficult—

gender floats through early memory to make the woman not
a woman and the back not a back but a resolute and highly tuned life
comb beginning

It was her mother's best friend. Or the men gathered
at a bamboo table with after dinner coffee hot

Each early puddle and stepping over it and stopping

Eroticism of wholeness

Rachel Moritz : SUBTRACTION (ATTIC NEWSPAPERS)

These pale brittles like instants
of elevation fall off their map

Structure pocks After a train
departs the courtyard rows

of abandoned suitcases lapse
And a man walks down the snowy

corridor where no one moves
except him covering absence

Remnant flutters beneath our
aerial A miniature survivor story

Gopher heads pop the insulated
yellow opening now to see these

paper bits embedded Nails as
survey-tags Our maps lose tracked

location One only secondary
structural task Releasing the beams

from their embedded time trek
I fold remaining newspapers

into a muffled ladder Climb
Then collapse my ladder

to a disappearing house Up
the gelid underside duration

tacks What suspends me
inside is not heat

Rachel Moritz : HOUSE IGNITES

Where bitter sea dries inside match-
Box as Mouse scuds to his den
& Daughter flees her sparking perimeter—

Why go? Waves will only bend train
Tracks and rungs will light, fire
Themselves upward: then heat pump,
Woolen whistle, will black-
Blanket sea, pressing her
Skin into one crisp

Note: there was no train from
His house, so fumble, Mouse
Before you wade

        delicately

            out—

Fig. 1.

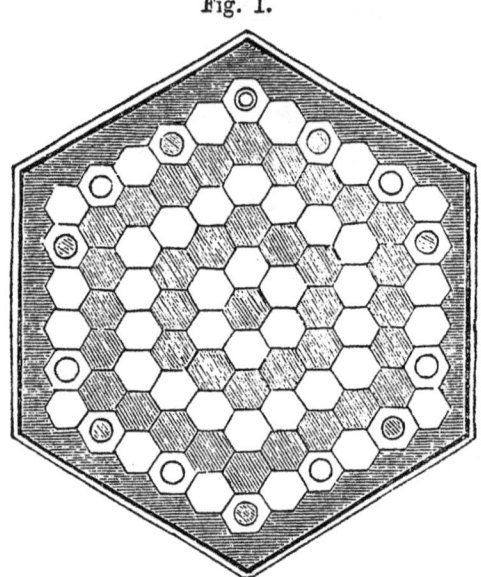

READY TO COMMENCE THE GAME.

Fig. 2.

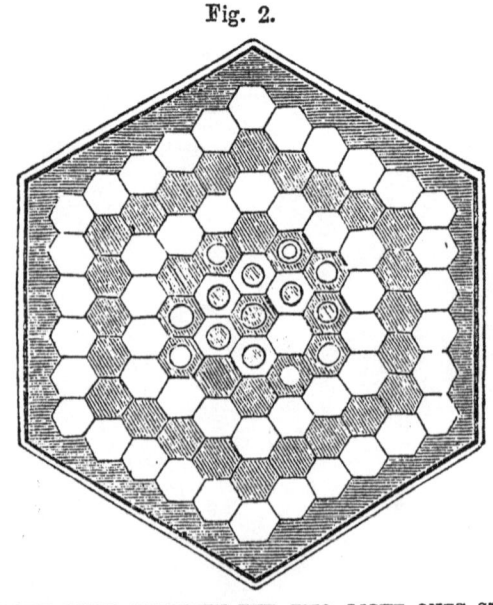

THE DARK PIECE BETWEEN THE TWO LIGHT ONES STANDING IN A RIGHT LINE MUST BE PUT BACK.

Fig. 3.

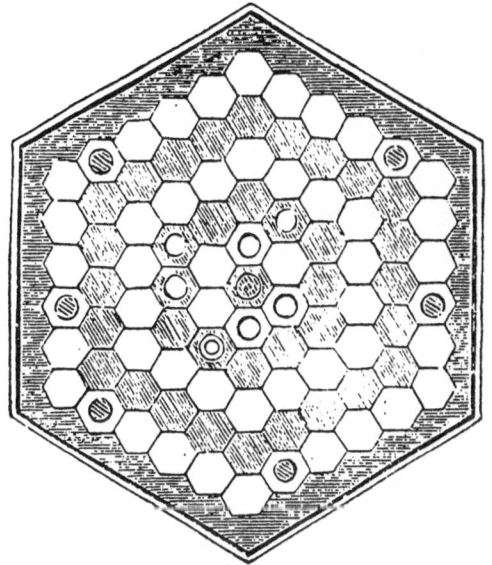

THE DARK QUEEN, BEING IN A RIGHT LINE BETWEEN TWO
LIGHT PIECES, MUST RETIRE.

Fig. 4.

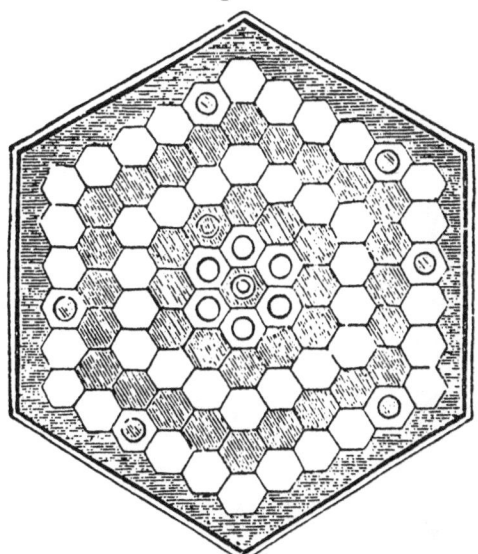

THE GAME WON BY THE LIGHT PIECES.

Simone Muench : ELEGY FOR THE UNSAID

after Neruda

In this mouth I gather darkness, an aria,
rosewater tongue, tympanic bone,
a poem more quiet than quietness,
a bronze song, something undone, salvia,
a crushed butterfly.
It is the blood on a light bulb, the seventh sadness,
a fluctuation that closes oceans and eyes.
The vermilion and solitary luminary
shimmies and singes the feathers of the aviary.

Moon, the clock's word, dear mother, ruin, rain.

Simone Muench : FREEZE FRAME, WITH FORSYTHIA

You will bind me
in an aquarelle, my skin
blue as Canterbury bells. Call me
mademoiselle before you execute, like the hand-
tinted photo of the dancer, Margarete Gertrud Zelle, arms
scissoring the air, fending bullets and flowers as she pirouettes.

You will find me
in the zero hour sipping
a whiskey sour with a cherry, my hair
yellow, not sallow or frizzed like Bishop's flower.
In a bell-shaped dress trimmed in snow-white florets, I smell
of fever, soil as I pose in the doorcase. You refer to me as daughter

of gnawed bones.
I am property of _____.
A profile in the slanted rain. I am
versatile. You call me Lily of the Nile, fingering
umbels as you scour the floor in search of my shadow. Hours
sift and flow and form a canted frame where you lean on one elbow

statuesque as a window
sash. You've captured me,
you say, mid-bloom, in your eye
frame, in the process of photograph and pose
and polyphonic prose, the kitchen lit by my ante-
bellum skirt, the yellow spikes of forsythia going up in flame.

Mark Neely : HISTORY OF US

Something about driving and we are
leveling Ohio hills, a safe distance
from the simmering sky.

Something about a quick drink
and our barstools swivel inward,
folding us together like a predator's wings.

Something about the city that makes us sparkle
through its glassy corridors,
looking for a story to fill a day.

Something in the water (or the gin)
to explain our beached blueprints,
our washed-out afternoons.

Something in the river that looks like us,
two alligators floating side-by-side.
No, turns out I'm just a log.

Something of the circus trainer in both of us,
not afraid to use the whip, something
of the lion, too tame to fight it out.

Something about changing where
to why, faster than a coffee cools,
then on to who, as quietly as hands.

Something about an exit and we're off,
out into the true temperature,
field fumes, the truer air.

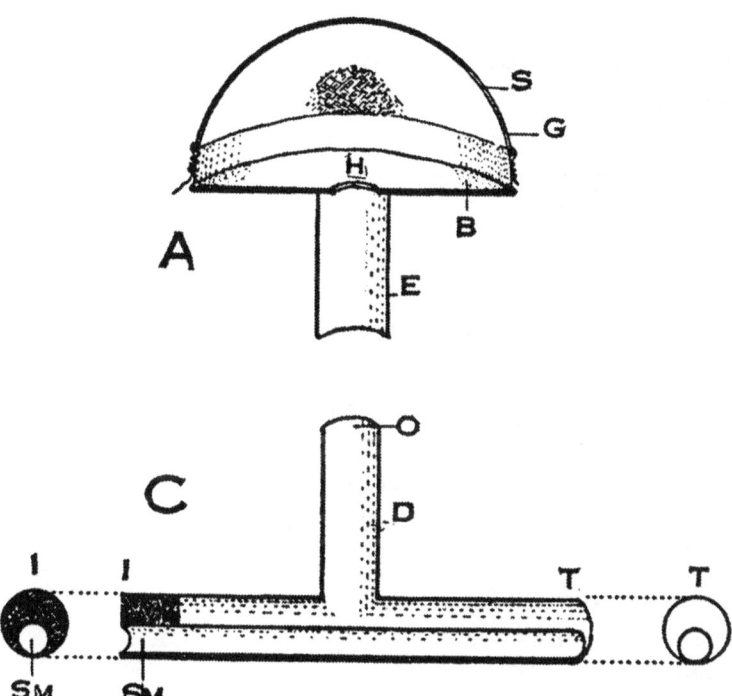

FIG. 1. *A*, anesthetic cone; *B*, circular base; *C*, cannula; *D* and *E*, intake and outlet tubes; *G*, gauze; *H*, hole into intake tube; *I*, end for attachment to artificial respiration apparatus; *O*, opening; *S*, wire screen; *sm*, small tube; *T*, trachea end of cannula.

Lindsay Packer : FILAMENTS, MASSES, COLONIES

come into the great world
bearing the old house of food
as the bean does.
cast off the old house amid better food.
find your supply of nourishment
even in the dark, fresh breeze of unseen atoms.

we shall begin our journey in the region of the great lakes and
the st lawrence river valley in the northern forest
where it broadens out and extends
from the atlantic to the pacific ocean.

foresters call this the boreal (boh-ree-al)
and this is the method bird students use.

coniferous wood, wide valleys
a two-meter thick layer
along the streamline

to many people, there is nothing interesting about the woods

did you pass by trees?
what kind were they?
perhaps you're one of those people
who just doesn't notice things.
the black, soft earth, the ferns and mosses
and the fungus plants

lichens are sometimes called mosses and
are the plants that grow on fences.

tall, straight trunks serve as stays,
just as ribs are to leaves.
generally stalks and trunks stand up of themselves,
but there are some which cannot.
these are called vines.

what birds to expect.
what varieties are suitable for shady areas?
others may be objectionable because their roots clog sewers.
be sure to make note of the general condition of each one as
good, fair, or poor.

Pedro Ponce : COMMERCIAL INTERRUPTION

An accident has occurred. The accident is no cause for alarm. Unanticipated events have led to unintended consequences. All evidence has been removed to an undisclosed area so that authorities may conduct a thorough investigation of the accident. Until the investigation is complete, authorities will not comment on the circumstances leading up to or the possible causes of the accident. Since the effects of the accident are most likely negligible, the investigation will itself be negligible, a matter of routine. The negligible investigation of this negligible accident may result in minor disturbances. These disturbances will be less distressing if curtains are drawn and the volume on entertainment consoles is adjusted accordingly. Speak loudly and clearly when addressing spouses, children, and pets. Make use of any stockpiled food as egress from homes has been temporarily prohibited. Units have been dispatched to monitor compliance with this temporary measure. Your compliance is appreciated for the duration of this temporary, negligible, accidental interruption.

Joshua Poteat : MEDITATION FOR THE DEAD SWISS

There is nothing more normal than the Swiss. There is no reason for them to die, so they are more terrifying in a way. They are us.
—Christian Boltanski

This much we understand: the desire of
    not wanting to die, of avoiding death
as much as possible. Which is the same.

Which is: how it rises, how it widens.

I low, if the winds drag another shutter open
    then it is only air that holds us above the billow
of clotheslines: chimney-slant, open-winged.

And if this is the end, hand us a blanket
    and sing about the city, its smoke of brick
and knife fights on the wharves.

This we understand: each thing is of itself.

Each thing is its end.

In the cupped palm of a cup: at the corner
    of corners: in the light of light: we stand
on roofs in the rain and watch the clouds move
    through the city because it is this that lets us move on.

The delicate map of breath on a window
    is no longer ours when it leaves us.

The skin of a plum, the inside of a mouth.

We hang on so tight to them our fingers
   mold into their shapes and we become them:

a violin's case open and empty,
   a cloth to wipe the sweat, the rosin.
Penciled marks to remember
   where to pause, where to end…

You and I, we want the same thing, the same ending.

   And in this wanting lies a failure
to see clearly, straight to the thing,

   to the light that illuminates us
on the street, crouching low
   against the walls of a pub in a strange country.

Maybe Switzerland, maybe not.

Either way, we are drunk in the rain.
   The knives in our pockets begin to sing
and we know the cobblestones are not ours,
   the doors to the barrel-maker's warehouse
are open but they are not ours

and the want bursts in our pockets
   like a plum as we sit and mumble
about the weather, about our lives.

And we hate each other for not dying.
   And for dying.

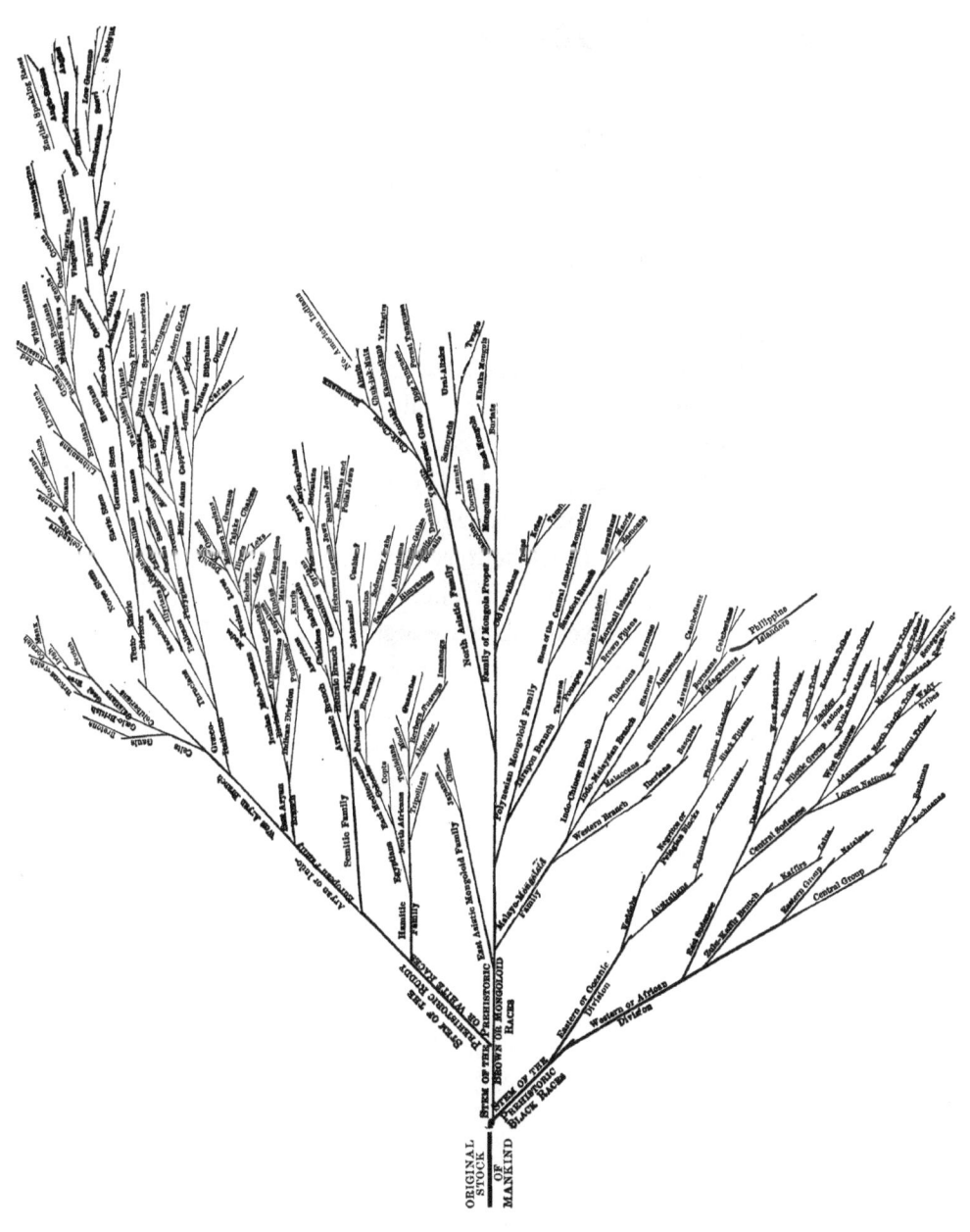

Billy Reynolds : ELEGY FOR A SMALL CANVAS

Without end, in all kinds of inner weather,
cloud-drifts, heartsick blue, off-again, on-again
drizzle, the sound of a tarp on grass a welcome
weight, a welcome sound to my ears, the faint,
almost over sound of the crickets, still there,
not quite through with us yet, all the small leaves
holding on until the last, cigarettes aglow,
stare, pace, lean, flick ash into the oil
drum around which my grandfather's help
warmed their hands, intimacies of cold weather,
ordinary dirt and ordinary staring,
the ordinary birth of each solitary breath,
the moon like the rim print of a heel in wet sand,
last year's nest next year's absolute best guess,
need a high priority: word spread fast.

Billy Reynolds : HUNGER

A kind of intimacy came about by August,
reading out loud to John. "The Shirt Poem"
got a quizzical look, "Baja" a nod,
the poetry a part of some larger hunger.
Like the boys who took to the old graveyard
with baseball bats. Like John trying to repair
each stone with epoxy. Like the young finch
blown from its nest, one of its wings missing,
a birth defect. I still remember it
as I first saw it, dragging itself
around that pine while I gawked, nothing to do
for it, or so I thought, but still
I wondered if I could have saved a life.
All summer I saw its body,
bits of bone and wing and then soil.

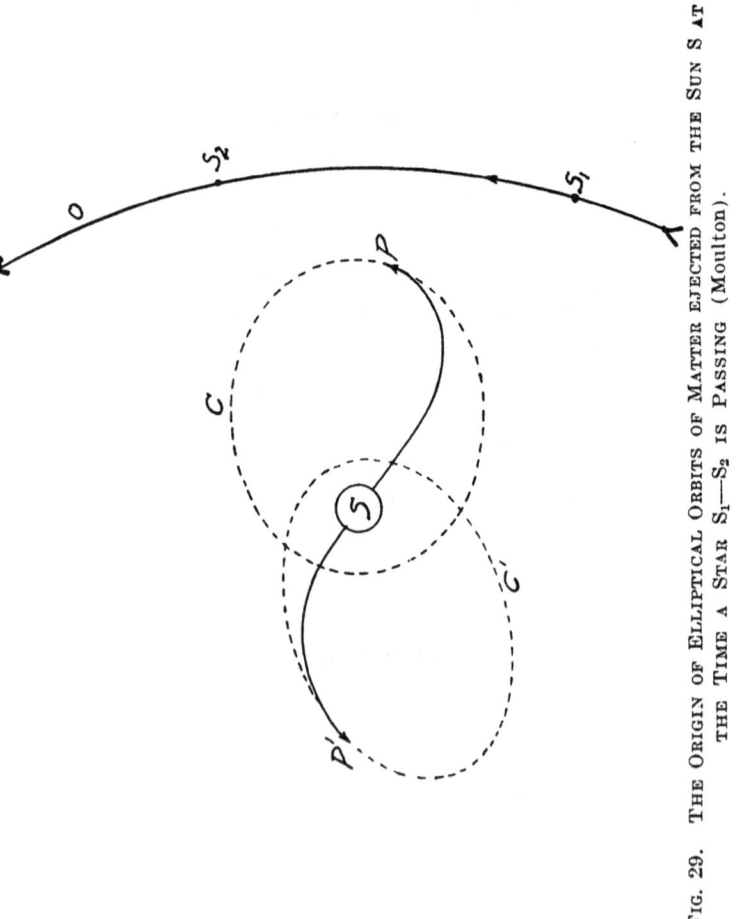

Fig. 29. The Origin of Elliptical Orbits of Matter ejected from the Sun S at the Time a Star S_1-S_2 is Passing (Moulton).

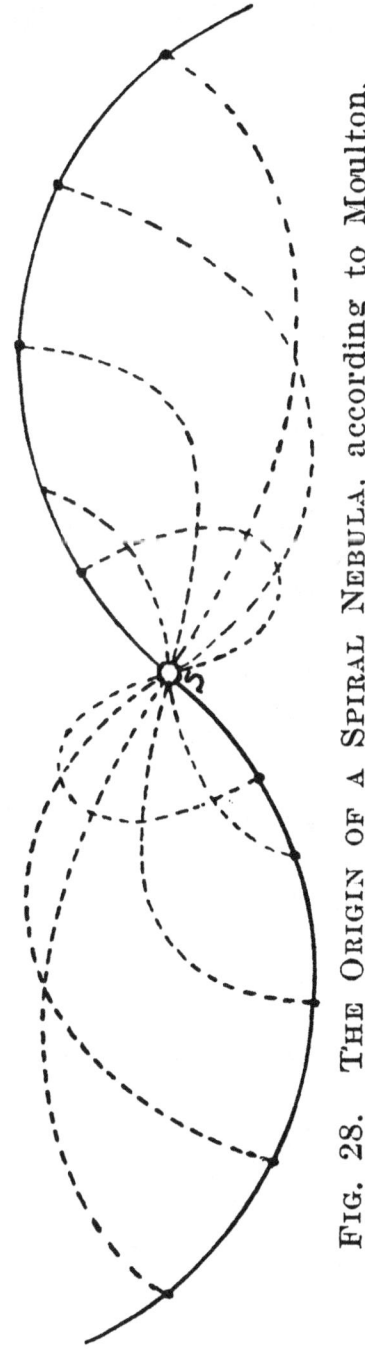

FIG. 28. THE ORIGIN OF A SPIRAL NEBULA, according to Moulton.

Mary Ann Rockwell : THE AGONIES OF INNOCENCE

Pooh, though Bear-of-Very-Little-Brain,

still figured out how far the charms of half-thought

and puddle-jump logic could hurl a boor

like him: there is mojo in the tongue-scoured

honey-pot; there is mercy dropped on real twits.

And so, despite the daily calamity

of poor judgment—the licked-clean gift,

the panicked fur impaction of the rabbit-

hole—he fumbles forth, relatively fearless,

certain that his next act will be caught, mid-spill,

by some sage, sandy-haired boy wearing shorts

and girls' shoes. And the seven-year-old,

with each fresh save, hoists up his burden of love,

heaves his thirteenth sigh, being daisy-chained so.

Michael J. Rosen : GEORGIC: ON LIVING FENCES

The deer wend their paths amid the woods,
plotting a narrow, single-file path
among the brambles, blockading trees, barbs
of wire, blackberry, and wild rose.

You take their lead, placing your inarticulate
feet over the quotes their hooves have printed:
paired half-moons some other, earlier nation
had scrawled to tell its travels to the future.

With chainsaw, mower, and leather gloves you clear
a wider swath, so you can walk erect
and without ducking, without mangling yourself
among the rampant multiflora roses

that are no more native to this place than you,
a virulent hybrid merchandized to farmers
fifty years ago as living fences,
feckless spires of predacious thorns

to keep the deer from the crops, the livestock from harm.
But now they do not border your fallow acres;
they have become them: within, without, wanted,
unwanted, are one and the same.

Mornings as you trace these paths you've added
to your maintenance list, you place your waffled soles
among the deer's notations: Fear, the pheromones
of the dogs that always accompany you

as if they served more than your childlessness,
the practice rounds—year-round—of neighbors' guns—
these haven't changed their common story a jot.
Perhaps they know no other ending; hapless

as this sounds to you, some season far,
or not so far from now (not that deer
can sense the difference), you could find yourself
following their worn and silent example.

When there is nowhere to escape
all the paths will lead there.

Michael J. Rosen : GEORGIC: ON BLOOD

Try: you might find consolation
   by citing "law of nature,"
an obligatory course
   of study you'd undertaken in your youth
and merely forgotten like so many
   foreign tongues you longed to master.

Likewise, you may be inclined
   to see this mole, the cat's first catch
(first, that is, you chanced to see),
   as beneficial, considering
the minions whose tunnels monogrammed
   your lawn in scorched, browning loops.

Yet this baby robin splayed
   upon the welcome mat, maimed
but not yet dead, is harder to dismiss:
   both cat and bird are fledglings
in their different elements,
   as you are when it comes to blood.

Friends will urge you to see these victims
   as tributes the cat is offering you.
Try that as well. Think all you like
   about the eggs pilfered from nests,
nests flung from swaying boughs,
   hatchlings swallowed by snakes, starved

by siblings, snatched in flight by hawks—
    causes you deem natural, beyond
the confines of your yard and conscience.
    But this one that your housecat wounds,
that she delivers into your field
    of vision, must this one be your charge,

sanctioned within your heart just like
    its killer, the once-stray cat?
You wrap the bird in a paper bag
    and end its suffering, not yours,
with the stomp of your heel—which summons the cat,
    and, instantly, your anger rises

as you lunge toward this beast you shelter,
    allow to curl against your shoulder
at night as if she were your dreams'
    familiar, and yet, you understand,
the moment you seize the scruff of her neck,
    you have no lesson to teach. Or learn.

Is it harder knowing there's nothing
    you can do, or that this death
is nothing, nothing more or less
    than your own cat's blank stare:
green with a core of darkness
    where you, too, must be reflected.

F. Daniel Rzicznek : VISITING A GRAVEYARD IN MARTINS FERRY

A dead bee clasps to a dandelion
where I spit in the broken grass.
White petals flood around my feet
and I am lost to the high stones.

A birdhouse teeters toward heaven
on a slant of rusty pole.
A safehouse among the dead,
protruding from the midst of a grave

as if anchored in the socket
of a faded sleeper's hungry skull.
The walls are stained and rough.
Warm straw pokes through the hole.

Something with feathers lives inside,
something filled with cold rain
and a song made of green glass
waiting to break.

F. Daniel Rzicznek : DRIVING, I THINK OF SPRING

I try to envision two months from now:
us, in Martins Ferry, maybe ambling
along rows of fractured headstones

or nursing lagers at Dutch Henry's
after visiting the tattoo parlor.
The flowers will have just discovered

their red and yellow paper ears,
still bound in tight green packages.
I can see us close on a bench

outside the library, admiring a sweet
lull in the conversation between us,
punctuated by the jabber of birdsong.

But in this cold nighttime I'm weary,
ready to pull off my shoes and call you.
Swirls of orange fog leap up behind me.

A snow truck flies past like a demon,
its black plow kicking sparks
that arch and bloom towards April.

F. Daniel Rzicznek : MESSAGE FROM A STRIP MALL

Out here,
where dumpsters string out
like beggars on a breadline,
the rain begins.

Pick-up trucks pace by, men
inside sneering at my broom,
dustpan, my corporate nametag.
I want to arch my neck and hiss
like the geese who nest
in the parking lot shrubbery
and beat their dark wings
at the traffic swerving around them.

When I try to sweep
the spilled trash, it will not stay
together. Some styrofoam pellets
roll to the asphalt's edge.
The world seems to reach
a unanimous conclusion
that I cannot know.
The rain will be coming
down a long time.

Zachary Schomburg : SEA OF JAPAN

Ichi. You have the Sea of Japan all over your face. *Ni, San.* I seemed to have left my Sea of Japan on the nightstand at your mother's place last night. When she called me this morning, she was excited to tell me about her new death trap (Sea of Japan). *Yon.* If floating in the Sea of Japan won't kill you, I will. *Go.* In last night's ball game, the pitcher was the Sea of Japan. And in the seventh inning it turned its attentions inward. It found everything to be black there. It wouldn't let anyone have the baseball. *Roku, Nana, Hati.* There was nothing behind the curtain except for some great Seas of Japan and a few thousand Seas of Japan. Then behind the Seas of Japan were giant-sized business executives controlling everything, including laughter. *Kyuu, Juu.* What I need to pick up at the store: clouds, a few thousand skulls, faces of old ghosts in the clouds, plastic poolside slide, plastic clouds, human ghosts haunting ghosts of bears, winter ghost clothes, a bigger fridge for T, plastic Sea of Japan, the Sea of Japan.

Zachary Schomburg : THE THINGS THAT SURROUND US

The entire world was there. The magnetic north pole was there. Prince Patrick Island was introduced to Prince of Wales Island and these were not the only islands being introduced to other islands. One room was completely filled with the space around all the islands. When you asked me if I was an island I told you that I was not. When you asked me to join you in the drawing room, I told you that I could not, that I was in fact an island and that I couldn't join anyone anywhere. Saddened and resigned, you revealed to me that you were not the two things that jut outward into the sea as I had assumed, but the little bit of gray sea between them. Then I told you I was actually the entire Arctic Ocean sometimes.

Eric Schwerer : QUINTESSENCE

Uncle Bimmy lived up Breakneck
in a doublewide that sat out back
the property of Grandpa Heck.

He'd flick his cigarette then smack
a stick against the fence line and
we'd come zinging up the lot.

Kneeling in the pungent dust
the evening cast about his home
he'd drag the heavy stone off

the well—we'd gather round—creep
closer—peering down—as one
good hand stirred away the webs

knit above the dankness. He'd speak
of vapor that wasn't vapor—
of smoke that stunk like breath—like hell

—the spore of something smoldering—
a seething in the hole. He'd say
this is what we must inhale

to understand our kin. We ran
—but one—alone I put my mouth
to pipe—that rusting way in.

Alan Semerdjian : ON ARMENIAN TRANSLATION

For instance,
to turn off a light
switch
is inevidently
not to close
like a book
of history
or a country
off from another
such as *kohtseh*

      "How do you close a light, Alan?"

say it: *koh* short *o* like
in fast policeman,
officer of the law
and government
agent of change,
and *tseh* like saying *it's a*
really fast.
The sound is respiratory,
is in/out,
lip puck then shut
the light,

      "that's how"

but the truer one—the subject at hand—
and the problem with translation
is that it's
too literal a turn to lead to off,

like a corner
or a getaway car,
a tunnel in a wall
under a city,
or the turn of a screw,
like reverse with *tartsur*,
so that it's a
"How do you reverse the light?"
rather than turn it off so much
that it has to be close.

How do you reverse the light?

Just close the light, please.

Alan Semerdjian : NEW AND DARKER GOLD IN THE PULPITS OF NIGHT

for Helen Hondropoulos

Things associated with loneliness.
Things associated with love.
Things like reruns.
Things appreciating solemnity.
Things almost melancholy.
Things in front of me.
Things that you would think are behind.
Things left behind.
Things that should be forgotten.
Things left in a flower bag behind the tree where she works.
Things that sound like holy.
Things that are holy and sound like shit.
Things like game shows.
Things like relationships like game shows.
Things you can't turn off.
Things you never wanted to turn off.
Things you knew you would never want to turn off
but you did.
Things you want off.
Things afraid of change.
Things in love with change.
Things afraid to love change.
Things like a pyramid.
Things in love with your ex-girlfriend.
Things in love with her letter H
and ancient civilizations.
Things that launch a thousand ships.
Things in love with Joyce Dewitt.

Things that are in secret.
Things that no one is supposed to know.
Things like telling secrets.
Things like feeling secure after telling secrets.
Things like a sermon.
Things like a sermon of secrets traded in for gold.
Things that begin with the letter T.
Things that are mistaken.
Things approaching forgiveness.
Ready. Go.

			1st	2d	3d	4th	5th	6th	7th	8th	9th
Minimals of 5 Good Years	Minus	Minimals of 5 Rust Years	−1.76	+8.50	+6.72	+7.70	+2.84	+7.24	+8.32	+1.42	+2.94
Maximals of 5 Rust Years	Minus	Maximals of 5 Good Years	−1.54	+9.16	+4.96	+4.48	+0.28	+5.74	+5.72	+4.10	+0.72

TABLE VIII

Salary of Assistant Professor
(compiled from various sources)

	Year	Minimum	Maximum	Average	Year	Minimum	Maximum	Average
California	'89			1,800	'07			1,620
Chicago					'09	2,000	2,500	2,102
Clark					'07			1,650
Columbia [10]	'88				'07			2,201
Cornell	'89			1,760	'07			1,715
Harvard		2,000	2,500		'07			2,719
					'09	2,500	3,000	1,851
Illinois					'07			1,083.33
Indiana	'89	1,200	1,800	1,400	'09	1,000	1,300	1,418
Iowa					'09	1,100	1,800	1,344
Johns Hopkins					'07			1,250
Kansas	'89	2,000	2,500	1,050 [11]	'09	1,000	1,500	1,827
Leland Stanford Jr.	'91			2,250	'08	1,500	2,500	1,624
Michigan					'07			1,791
Minnesota	'89	800	1,350	1,162.5	'09	1,400	2,400	1,800
Missouri					'09	1,500	2,000	1,500
Nebraska					'07			1,850
Pennsylvania					'07			1,824
Princeton					'07			1,425
Virginia					'07			1,733
Wisconsin	'89	1,100	1,500	1,250	'09	1,500	2,500	2,100 [12]
Yale	'88	1,750	2,500	1,900	'09	1,800	2,500	

Ron Singer : THE ACTUARIALIST

PROSPECTUS

Brandon Flicker (GradCertActSt, MActSt), President and CEO, Actuarialist Life Solutions, Inc.™
brflk@actlife.com

1. Introductory

Note : Since prospective clients who read this brochure are unlikely to recognize the term "actuarialist,"™ I offer the following definitional and biographical notes to enhance transparency and to establish my *bona fides*.

1A. Definitional

What, then, is an actuarialist™? In layman's terms, using the same stochastic and other statistical models as an actual actuary, an actuarialist offers consultations to private parties which provide accurate data relevant to specific plans and dreams, including, where relevant, data for life expectancy. The actuarialist thereby facilitates realistic estimates of clients' chances of bringing said plans and dreams to fruition, with or without considerations of mortality.

1B. Biographical

In 2002, after a nine-year stint in the insurance "game," which followed immediately upon graduation from college, nine years which constituted my entire, unique opportunity to experience, for better or worse, the state of being a twenty-something ... *I had had it!* Nine years of brain-frying study through a series of eleven grueling examinations which together brought me to maximum rank and salary in what has been rated the first or second-most desirable profession (ha!) in this, our great nation. Nine years of significantly bloating the bottom line of a major conglomerate (the name-brand recognition of which I will not now enhance by either identification or excoriation) which specializes in annuities and in property and casualty insurance. Nine years of stochastically calibrating rates for policies ranging from property and liability for a large, modern, wooden vacation structure with concrete-block foundation and no cellar, eight-hundred yards from the ocean in an environment of moderate-to-high hurricane activity; to a term annuity with survivors' rights for a fifty-something who is currently fit and practicing a healthy lifestyle, but who smoked cigarettes (an average of 1.7 packs per day, filtered) from age sixteen until he suffered a minor infarction at forty-one, and whose family tree features on both primary branches rates of smoking-related lung cancer and coronary disease which are of statistically significant elevation. In short, to repeat, *I had had it!*

Inasmuch as my present purpose is only incidentally biographical, having just sketched in the years of my life from ages 22 to 30 (by which point my remaining life expectancy was 46.4), I will stint even further upon the intermediate steps: the personal crisis which precipitated my resignation; the terms of said resignation (*i.e.*, the gold-plated parachute); my motives for entering, or rather for inventing, my current profession (independence and altruism); and all financial and logistical details of my current operation other than the fee structure delineated in **Section 3** (see below) of this prospectus.

2. Examples

Note: In order to provide prospective clients with some sense of the parameters of what an actuarialist can and cannot do,

I offer four examples of consultations performed for previous clients (**2.1-2.4**) and one (**2.5**) which was designed, but not carried out.

Disclaimers:

Before proceeding to these examples, however, I must issue the following three disclaimers, the first two adapted in paraphrase from the **Exposure Draft of October 15, 1999, International Actuarial Association**, and the third, a caveat suggested by counsel as standard practice:

—**Principle 3.5. Avoidance of Failure:** For most risk-management estimates with specified success criteria, there is a set of parameters such that a combination of values of the probabilistic criteria reduces the failure probability, as estimated by a valid actuarial model, to below a specified positive level.

—**Principle 3.6. Degree of Actuarial Soundness:** For most risk-management estimates, there is a set of parameters such that a combination of values produces a degree of actuarial soundness, as estimated by a valid actuarial model, that exceeds a specified level less than one.

—**Caveat:** The examples which follow are intended solely to illustrate prior practice, and are not intended for use in any way, shape or form in the creation of plans or dreams by readers of this prospectus. In light of **Principles 3.5** and **3.6** supra, any reader who attempts to use directly, or to extrapolate from, said examples, does so at his or her own risk. In that event, **Actuarialist Life Solutions, Inc.**™ shall incur no legal liability whatsoever. In other words, don't try these in your own home or office!

Example 2.1. A 62-year old, six-foot tall, physically fit, diet-and-exercise-conscious, highly successful, black male advertising executive in excellent health, aside from very mild age-related scoliosis and a history of hypertension and diabetes on the maternal branch, asked whether the Norfolk pine in his living room, currently 5'10" high and just sprouting its newest layer, will outgrow him.

client's life expectancy (factored for likelihood of continued good health and for median life expectancy for African-American males age 62, 84.4): 85.39

mean growth rate of Norfolk pines: one layer every 1.17 years

mean height of each layer of this particular tree: four inches (4")*

* Strictly speaking, this number, 4", refers to the height of the section of the tree's stem between all produced, but not necessarily remaining, layers, since lower layers tend to fall off, especially in unhealthy trees, such as those which have been traumatized by events like ceiling collapse.

actuarialistic assessment of likelihood of pine outpacing man: barring unforeseen disease of, or accident to, tree, as close to certain as anything in this world can be.

advice to client: Count on it.

comment: In one way, this consultation was anomalous, since the client appeared to seek the information for no purpose other than some obscure mental or emotional satisfaction

Example 2.2. A client in the 98th percentile for wealth, but with no other relevant demographic characteristics, asked me to determine the likelihood that the marriage of his daughter and only child (white, Episcopalian, age 20) to an immigrant from a war-torn African nation on his last year in the U.S. on a student visa (black, Baptist/animist, age ?27) will end in divorce, and, if so, the likelihood that this divorce will occur before or after the couple has produced a child or children.

divorce rate from American wives for all males of this man's nationality (i.e., "tribe") on student visas in U.S: data unavailable

divorce rate from American wives for all males from this man's country on student visas in U.S.: 27% (est. margin of error: 12%)

mean duration of all terminated marriages: 5.6 years (est. margin of error: 12%)

mean time elapsed between marriage and production of (first) child in all terminated marriages: 2.6 years (est. margin of error: 12%)

other relevant data: the client has, himself, been divorced six times; his daughter's mother, twice; 87% of all members of the client's family have been divorced at least once, as have 63% of all members of his daughter's mother's family; in 94% of all divorces on both sides, an average of 2.4 children were produced prior to divorce and, in only 0.73 per cent, no children.

advice to client: The worst-case scenario (divorce after the production of a child or children) seems virtually certain. Deal.

caveat to client: [**See Principle 3.6. Degree of Actuarial Soundness** (*supra*)]. On the 0-1 scale, this prediction achieves only 0.347. To approach 0.750, the generally acceptable level of soundness in cases such as these, where the human factors are, alas, somewhat indeterminate, one would have to garner information relevant to at least two further *random variables*: cultural attitudes toward marriage and divorce within the groom's particular nationality, and divorce rates within both the groom's nuclear and extended families. Although obtaining both sets of information would be possible, the task would require at least two subcontractors: a private investigator within, or with access to, the groom's home country; and an anthropologist (cultural) cognizant of patterns of marriage and divorce within the groom's nationality. After a short deliberation, the client decided not to sign a second contract for these additional services. Quote: "No, that's okay, I get the picture."

Example 2.3. A farmer (truck and dairy) who depends for a significant proportion of his income on an elaborate, well-maintained farm stand which is situated directly beside the road just to the left of his large (3000 cubic-foot) barn asked for a cursory (*i.e.* inexpensive) study of whether he should repaint the sides and back of the barn as well as the front. It was a given that the barn needed painting. It was also a given that the *degree of actuarial soundness* he could expect from this study would be commensurate with the cost. In other words, the *stochastic model*, in this case, would be by no means deterministic.

principal determinant (1): comparison of sales volumes at farm stands proximate to buildings painted, unpainted, and partially painted. The ratio is 1 to .4 to .7 .

principal determinant (2): cost of painting ($1700) and of partially painting ($950)* said barn.

* Given that the farmer has no children or other relatives

residing in the area from whom he might extract free or barter labor, and given that both he and his wife "already have our hands full," $1700/$950 were the (sole) estimates for the job, as provided by two young, moderately experienced local men who are reputed to be honest, capable, and in possession of all necessary equipment.

actuarialistic estimate: the most cost-effective solution would be to paint only the front of the barn plus the side visible from the stand (the left side, from the vantage of the road and the entrance to the stand). Fortunately, the other (right) side faces an impenetrable grove of alders. It was also estimated (by intuition) that almost no customers who happen to wander around behind the barn to "sightsee" are likely to be deterred by the unpainted back of the barn from purchasing the produce, dairy products, jams and baked goods for which this farm stand is renowned

advice to client: Get the boys out there before the weather (fair and cool) and the season (late-August) turn.

conclusion: This was one of my favorite consultations. Since the barn was (partially) repainted two years ago,** sales from the stand, rather than declining, have actually increased 1.7% p.a.***

Furthermore, since my own country house is located in the vicinity (2.8 miles) of the farm, I was pleased to waive my fee in favor of three summers' supply of "any and all products sold at —— Farms which can reasonably be construed as meeting the normal needs of a bachelor and temperate eater." In line with the **Caveat** (**Section 2. Introductory**), however, readers of this prospectus should instantly disabuse themselves of any notion they may have conceived to the effect that my services could ever again be obtained on anything but a strictly cash basis.

(See **Section 3. Fee Structure**, below.)

** actually costing, in the event, $936.28, or $13.72 *below* estimate.

*** Professional standards compel me to point out, however, that unexamined *random variables* render absurd any assertion of a causal relationship between the paint job and the increase in sales.

Example 2.4. A seventy-one year-old woman (white, in excellent health) asked me to determine whether she will have time to knit a sweater for her unborn grandchild before either she (the grandmother) dies or the world ends.

client's remaining life expectancy: 13.4 years

minimal "life expectancy" for Earth: 46 years.*

* Our best available estimate for the end of the world comes from the emerging science of econophysics, a movement among physicists which models economic systems using techniques and concepts initially developed to analyze the out-of-equilibrium dynamics of complex systems. Econophysicists have recently confirmed Sir Isaac Newton's famous Bible-based estimate that the world will end c.2050. The corroborating estimate is based upon a singular convergence of many long-term demographic, economic and financial series.

My own interest in econophysics dates from shortly after the severance of my corporate affiliation. Incidentally, econophysicists also predicted that the Nikkei would rise 50% in 1990 (it "only" rose 49%), and they have recently predicted that the U.K. housing bubble will burst no later than 2004.

client's projected time frame for project: 6-18 months

additional factor significantly impacting actuarialistic assessment of project's coming to fruition: Over the past two years, the client's daughter, 34, and the daughter's live-in "other" (male, 31) have mentioned with increasing frequency their desire to produce a child "soon."

advice to client: Pick a pattern, buy the wool. The "baby" will be in his/her forties by the time the world ends, by which time he/she will have outgrown this and, presumably, many other sweaters.

Example 2.5. A 31 year-old woman wished to discover the likelihood that her neutered eight year-old Tom cat will attack the man who has been her lover for one month, while the man is sleeping. The cat has already inflicted several superficial scratches and one small bite while the man was awake.

*No further data available**

* This consultation did not occur. Not that the question was by any means unanswerable, but in order to establish adequate *random variables* (*i.e.*, to assign numerical values to the likelihood of attacks of various severity and of a non-attack), and subsequently to quantify all *probabilistic outcomes* (*i.e.*, to assign a number between zero and one to the likelihood of attacks of various severity and of a non-attack), I estimated 20 hours of work at my usual fee of $180 per hour (see **Section 3**, below), whereupon the client decided not to proceed. In my own defense, let me explain that the *random variables* for this study would have been complex and subtle: for example, previous behavior by the cat toward prior boyfriends and any others who had been perceived (presumably) as rivals for

the client's affection; plus the time frame of attack patterns by cats—to wit, *longitudinal data* concerning the increase or decrease of jealousy aggression behavior among cats of various ages and sub-species—if such data even exist.

As a courtesy, and in order to effect closure, I suggested to this non-client the expedient of locking the cat in an empty room at such times as said boyfriend is on the premises, with the caveat that she not choose the bathroom, in case the boyfriend should happen to get up in the night.

3. **Fee Structure** (see attached pamphlet)

4. **Conclusion.**

On a personal note: suffice it to say that, since my private life is virtually synonymous with my professional one, I am now happy. Rashly ignoring any and all projected health factors and all projected local, national, continental, planetary or cosmic disasters, whether induced by humans or so-called acts of God, I expect to remain same (happy) for 44.4 more years* (based upon current life expectancy for 32 year-old white males in the U.S.).

* which, I note—not without a certain ambivalence—would bring me to A.D./C.E. 2048.

Marcus Slease : ICEBOX WITH HEART

Let the monks sing

proverbial food on the brink

a song of blustered English

foreign intuition

hot bricks in head.

The organ replaces the pom-pom.

The icebox contains a heart.

Bruce Smith : SONG OF THE SOULIST

I was a Soulist, blinking homunculus, with the buzz of the

    One end of the telephone was I

molecules making me sentimental, a ESP

    she was on the other end, my mother, measuring the ticks

of feeling coming from the memory of still photographs

    outraged at the cost of the long distance call, imagining

the mushroom cloud and nullifying atoms, seraphs

    patched-through communiqué from Iwo to Kwajalein to Philadelphia

in the background behind mother/father, one with downpours

    during the war when the gyrenes manned the switchboards

of light obliterating the faces or shadowing faces of the adored

    I was acquainted with the life and longing

I was a Soulist when I felt something

    prodigal in her estimation, impractical, interior

looking into the Grand Canyon that was maybe looking

    boy in her estimation, a profligate monk, decadence

itself and not I, not some subcutaneous blush

    of one who did not know the depression or did not make

of the languorous, a dreamy dream like the rush

    the sacrifice: the phone is the fetish of the hidden face

of the narcotic perfume of the real in musical

    hushed and belled like the egotistical sublime

or infantile forms: like the sheets thrown over the furniture (soulful)

    my feeling (coiled and choked back) or the grand enterprise

in foreign films (all that sad finale) or sheets over you:

    bandaged as the voices were crossed by

ghost or sham Klansman: artifacts of other than you

    radio where she subdued the Loas, the

white, Italian, English, something, the one-quarter Russian Jew

    Voodoo gods (of muggles and mood indigo, of shame and swoon)

you looked like a Korean

    she had to be the conscience of the

boy in the photos, a boy in his protean

body I inhabited like the zombie

forms of statue or satyr, playing war or base

　　　who went after the bitch goddess to the

ball: sampling a stance from the young Willie Mays

　　　paradise of fields where I worked

and so the soul was formed in Westfield, Alabama

　　　(I wanted a car and a vacation, was this too much

or in the dust of Puerto Rico, each occasion a drama

　　　to ask of a vocation?) My calling was

of becoming or inventing a feeling that dissolved

　　　measureless self and measureless other, nothing special

or feeling it, an amplitude or a terribilità that you later

　　　Later I learned it was my poverty that was

learned was Michaelangelo or a blow to the solar plexus, greater

　　　the reason I called, tangled as it was in her economy

than the sentiments of white flowers, the face of the first born,
or the smoky tenor

　　　and my need to sound the terrible unknowing

the cloud over a pond, the sea and New Jersey

    I felt in my acquaintance (I can't say life) the world

My heart sutra said (soulfully) there must be a fallacy

    I said the anecdote or incident, my testimony

to the pathetic hankering, the ash from the fire in the belly

    of untold secrets and the reflexive verbs

and your class warfare and your sympathies are spoils

    of fear about her and for me and fear

of soul. I pled allegiance to the rainbowed and oily

    of orphanhood. Before she hung up she extracted

cloud that floated free of mattering yet mattered to me

    promises of reflexive visits I resisted

I was a Soulist until I found myself smelling the honeysuckle

    Then she hung up and ended all my apostrophe

and loving my cozy place by the beautiful

    Mother Mambo, squeeze every O and corpuscle

while carving crosses on the foreheads of the infidels

    of slaves' blood from my veins.

Sara Jane Stoner : LACHRYMOSA

From behind, the driver's hair appears short, dyed black with dusty brown roots, the appearance both careless and careworn. The black sheen of the still-dyed hair looks more real than real against the mottled and torn gray of the ceiling, the dull white of the face.

The driver's cheek glistens wet in the late afternoon light, though it isn't raining—despite the fact that it's always raining in story cities, isn't it? But the skin is wet, as if the driver has been driving with their head hanging out the window, a joyous hound, heedless of the raindrops, even reveling in their acrid coolness.

But the latest sky report assures you: nothing but blue skies for months.

*

The meaning of the city is short like sentences today and noticeably darkened by the lofty pitch of the cloudless sky. The ground has been hollowed out for trains. The monuments of the city are blackened, though this has no effect on the buildings' ability to impress or be identified. Even at a distance, the city's pollution only heightens your satisfaction at the moment their façades part the curtains of smog to thunderous traffic noise.

However, you strive to ignore the quarter inch of grass stubble because it makes the city look dingy in its sad struggle for greenness. You are reminded of your unremarkable plodding to and fro, your incidental employment, your own history of bad dye jobs. Your mood is worsened by memories of healthy suburban yards swaddled in fence that begin to loosen in your head like aching teeth. Even the city's canines do not assuage this sudden pain; the dogs' panting, anticipatory joy at the stunted blades results in immediate waste. Somehow, the city smell of dog shit offers your mouth the added insult of a foul taste.

*

And if you haven't yet noticed, notice! She is crying, weeping, sobbing—tears everywhere so that the collar of her shirt is soaked and the fabric of her pants at her lap is damp. A hollow moan throbs in her chest, at a pitch something like warning.

She has driven through the streets, her ears aimed toward the closed doors of theaters, her radio tuned to the message, the never-ending herald of that perfect blast.

*

OUR LADY OF PERPETUAL ... BOMBING IN A NORTHERN NEIGHBORHOOD ... IRREPLACEABLE! ... EVERYONE BUT THE ONE WHO MATTERED ESCAPED ... ALAS, POOR ... ALAS ... THE SHATTERED GLASS OF THE EIGHTEENTH CENTURY.

*

And if she wore glasses they would be fogged; and if she were a cartoon, tears would spurt in geysers and pool at her feet; and her makeup would be miraculous, perfect; and if this were that kind of story, she would flood the car with the liquid volume of her pain and the tinny violins would play, and of course it would be raining—how else would the landscape express its compassion? If this were that kind of story. And if the city were prone to such hopeless fits of emotion.

*

First thing: she drives a taxi, one that you assumed when you called the service would be yellow but—never more wrong you are—it is pink. Though once it could have been red.

But you're in a hurry! You have that meeting, conference, signing, facial, social drinking, dinner, matinee, free day…Your wallet a proud bulk in your back pocket; your backpack a quiet child slumped on your lap; your purse a sliver of liberty wedged between your knees. Perhaps it rubs you a bit how your brown calfskin satchel cries "foul!" on the cracked burgundy leatherette—which pinches your legs even through the thick wool of your pants, whose fineness demands your constant vigilance and a travel iron—but at least she arrived quickly. You admire the fade of your jeans at the rounded cliffs of your knees. You spread your skirt across the seat in a romantic fan. You scratch at a crusty spot on your jogging suit. You are distracted by your own pants. You are in the back seat of a taxi that is headed, thankfully, in the right direction.

So when you lift your head and really take notice of the fact that you have a woman driving, as you give the address, careful to say "please," you finally see she is weeping, and think: she is weeping as women sometimes weep. She is taking care to check her blind spot and signal her return to traffic; and she is weeping.

And you wonder, despite your careful politesse, if your tone was rude. You smooth your lap with your palms, resolved that this display of emotion has nothing to do with you. All of this must have pre-existed your arrival in the cab. Indeed, something must be wrong with her, or something must have happened to her.

*

Imagine from above if you can, at cloud level, the city thrown like a holey net strung with stones, bits of glass, and cars that appear like gems. Those pale exhalations you expect to dissipate are plant life. The people of the city almost go missing from this height; they look smaller than ants and less persistent. You imagine that the city dogs who aren't tucked away in studio or townhouse or loft or hole are dead in the murderous streets, though you wouldn't be able to see them anyway.

At this distance, anyone can observe that the colorful human kinesis along the grid is undetermined—clever, but not confident—and little is different at night; only that the cars are reduced to the color of sparkling lights and the buildings simple stumps, freckled with glow. The monuments, of course, are rouged and lit for the stage.

But you will marvel at the roundedness of your body, ballooning thighs and toes hovering so large over the diminished city. This disorientation makes possible the foreshortening of buildings.

*

Remember that other people of the city drive past monuments, thinking, Oh that cathedral, Saint.. Something—perhaps it's a visit that they've always, for years, been meaning to make. As it is, they are quite friendly with the landmark, the exterior, though sometimes they are bored, you are bored, by the dimness of the stained glass windows from the outside.

People still expect that a bright glow from within will charm them as they pass, with no need for them to enter or grow silent.

*

She knew where you were going before you had to utter a word. From behind her, your weeping taxi driver, you imagine the full impact of her face before you: her look soft, or perhaps rather hard, with narrowed, swollen eyes and a mouth chapped by ragged breath, lips chewed through for fear or worry.

As it is, peeking over the seat and through the gap in the plexiglass, you can only make out her profile: a shiny curve of cheek. In the rearview mirror, so cracked as to be useless, you catch odd slices of her, blotches of red at her neck, around her nose and eyes, spoiling the apples of her cheeks.

You figure that she would probably look better if she weren't crying. And you hope, for her sake, that she didn't wear mascara today, and where is that travel pack of tissues you had in your purse? And of all the times to be tissueless; and so much for kindness, or even simple custom.

But who would actually accept a stranger's monogrammed kerchief, no matter how starched and bleached?

You think of her nose steadily, how tears and snot must run around her mouth and into it—but surely, as you dig through your bag, surely you must have a napkin left over from that recent indulgence, that quickie hot dog on the city corner. But you cannot offer her even the silliness of a wet nap. Instead you fish out the gel sanitizer and massage it into your hands.

Frankly, you are annoyed by all that blubbering up there in the front seat. Even if you aren't a parent, you feel like one in your search for tissues. Even if you aren't a therapist, you feel a sudden pressure to be helpful, to cross your legs at the ankles, to ask thoughtful, open-ended questions, to dispense benign advice. Even the daytime talk show dilettantes would catch a whiff of tragedy in the tight space of the cab, and just beyond this smell is fear.

*

As everyone knows, and has come to expect, there is murderous traffic in the city. It froths with maniacal honkers, surgers, cutters—professionals. Of these city drivers, most swear by the most offensive of offenses. Off the road, they calmly reason that inspiring fear among their fellow drivers will make everyone more vigilant behind the wheel, and therefore safer. Many stud their tires and protect themselves with bubbles of steel, massive vehicles that do most of the driving for them. The cars halt midway into intersections, swerve with the force of a cornering train, and carve S-curves into the putty of the pavement.

Despite all this careful planning and equipage, a great many "close" calls result in metal-on-metal groans. All across town, sirens chase the protests of shattered windshields. A legion of flame-retardant brooms clears the wreckage and its pool of gas. And the surviving drivers go on to buy new cars, bigger ones with stronger skeletons.

And there are those, like you, who simply will not drive, who have the luxury not to. Those who cover their eyes, who grope for their seatbelts without thinking or needing the warnings of mayoral placards or earnest movie stars. They know that skill is rare among the drivers of the city.

*

People ask less of skyscrapers, a launching upward of the eyes, a simple dizziness. On blue sky days a certain thrill. The city people nurse their disbelief until it grows up to be cynical. So the tall buildings are mostly left to themselves and their insistence on being so very vertical.

Because the truth is, in fact, the heights challenge you; sometimes, even the buildings' basic demand of you to look up! look up! is asking too much. Your neck aches and your eyes throb. Better to whiz by them in a jewel-toned sedan or a seasoned cab, forced only to reckon with the stacked floors that fit in the frame of the car's window, than have to struggle to fit the whole monster in your mind.

You prefer taxis to trains. You avoid the subterranean, its music, its hellish smells, the dark mouths of its corridors. No where to go to avoid the blackened city water gushing from a crack in the arch above the tracks in front of you. Nowhere to hide and so you cower from that pack of city children, their flashing eyes trap you where you stand. You cannot achieve enough distance to see them and still love them. Instead you always end up studying the slack and darkened pores of the man sitting next to you.

There are other excuses for your abandonment of the city's trains, but you often cite—on bad days—your crushing claustrophobia—on good days—your enjoyment of the city's surface, rendered in other people, glass, light, and commerce. The urgent messages of billboards.

The bustling.

*

The woman driving your cab now vibrates with a low, prehistoric moan, and you begin to think of hormones—their shrewd manipulation of woman into a crisis of gratuitous empathy. Nature's plot: a feminine inadequacy.

How many female cab drivers are there in this world?

In that way of women weeping, she reminds you of an ex-wife, an aging mother, a child, a war bride, a sick sister, a girlfriend you once abandoned in that museum in Rome.

But there is the strange fact of her driving. As the sobs shake her rounded back, you are awed by her smooth negotiation of the most violently clogged expressways. You are breathless at the assertive leap and dodge of the cab, masterfully gliding across three packed lanes, dropping down some previously undiscovered alley to emerge on an avenue mysteriously clear of cars. On asphalt given to sharp-edged, hippo-sized gaps, her steerage makes you believe you could sip that coffee so hot it deserves its own warning.

Her tears, rather than interfere with her vision, seem to make it more acute. You grip the door handle as she makes a microscopic correction, sparing the lives of straggling schoolchildren without sacrificing an ounce of speed. Such is her fearless negotiation of the walker-bound elderly, drunken stumblers, and horse-borne members of the police force. In fact, you see a cop actually canter along side her, perfectly parallel, and give an appreciative nod.

*

You have a prescription for this brand of sadness. You finger the bottle in your purse, briefcase, backpack, pocket; imagine the tangy rattle of that life-saving orange.

Now imagine sharing.

*

Be reasonable with yourself. Tell her: I AM SORRY FOR YOUR LOSS.

For what else but someone or something's death brings this depth of sorrow? The kidnapping of a beloved pet? Besides, you can imagine yourself mourning someone in your life. Certainly.

At the intersection, a hardened city driver in his chariot of glossy steel swivels toward your lady cab driver with a vigor suggesting a challenge, a race, a derby. You're struck suddenly by the urge to serve and protect. But you watch as her sodden, distorted face catches at his eyes behind his sunglasses. The driver raises them off his face and begins to interpret her tears:

a lost love, perhaps, a mugging, even a speeding ticket or a short fare—something he could imagine himself weeping over—something real. You see him looking at her and then he sees you, his eyes sharp and accusatory and wordlessly he decides that YOU ARE THE ASSHOLE WHO IS MAKING HER CRY.

You duck down then, pressing your knees into the driver's seat in front of you, until the city begins moving in the windows and once again you sense its profound ignorance of you.

*

And after the sympathy that you have imagined yourself into dries up, what is it that you believe she cries for? You can only nod and agree with her emotion like a bit of weather. Those in the high buildings of the city reach across the sky to shake hands on her sadness, as though it were an investment in the city they might be willing to take a risk on.

*

When she turns to look at you, to give you change, her wet face is clear, empty, transparent—through her the rain-covered city: the people with their umbrellas, splashing along the sidewalks and gutters behind her forehead. The street lights swollen into softer circles past her eyes and the damp fog at dusk, heavy and mauve. The buildings fade the higher they rise through the sheets of rain in her hair.

If she could talk, she might tell you a story about a woman who became an appendage of her taxi, an installation that was an upgrade perhaps, but still, a component. The wheel gripped her hands and began to direct her arms through an endless circular dance. Once upon a time, the woman woke to find herself in her taxi. Then night fell on her in her taxi. No matter where she went she ended up in the same place, and after a while she couldn't remember how she used to hold her children. The numbness in her lower lumbar region, the woman reasoned, was both due to the seat and the seat itself. And no pill or bottle could revive the good feeling like sunlight that she used to feel following her closely, warming her neck. Eventually, the woman didn't need mirrors anymore. She knew in her body when the taxi was clear or when she could back up no further.

And when she thought of those buildings—the "out of service" light just flickered on—how skyscrapers must tire of the sky. How they must wish to meet her and her pink cab down on the water by the pier, where she kept up her crying with the windows rolled down, waiting.

*

When she delivers you safely and her door slams home, the rushing of the air around you will remind you, suddenly, of falling. From the sidewalk you'll stand and watch her crest that bit of hill, funnel into the narrow bridge, pick up speed and pour into downtown. You imagine she will run uphill in rivulets, soaking the ground, and all the streets uptown will rise with a silent flood.

As you climb up your stairs or stand in your swift brass elevator, you'll find somewhere to file this vision away. Some dusty bin for the unusual. But when the rain returns, her story will slip out of your head. She will splash past you as you stand waiting on the street corner, a newspaper wilting above your head, and you will forget how to stiffen your arm to hail yourself a taxi.

Jay Surdukowski : WORD SEARCH

Like going to the vet, I wag and nudge,
paw your jacket before you leave me.
The terminal is steel and green.
You drive off slow as if it's a movie.

Nothing's so sad as a Midwest airport.
At the gate, the woman next to me
focuses intently on her word search;
she might be a substitute teacher
or a school lunch worker.
Her nose wrinkles mouselike at the clue,
Puzzle 79, words about "Garage Sales."
She has not circled any in a while.

In my plane reading, Robert Lowell
has just terrorized Bloomington,
screaming he was the Holy Ghost.
It took five Hoosier policemen
to restrain the poet while
some decent folk looked on.

The word searcher stares for a while,
she's circled one or two in an hour.
Is it refusal of error that breaks our life?
In the airport advertisement,
the bare chested boy nestles
into a girl's smooth shoulder.
They are the color of peach crayon.
Somewhere west, you drive home.
She finds the words one-by-one.

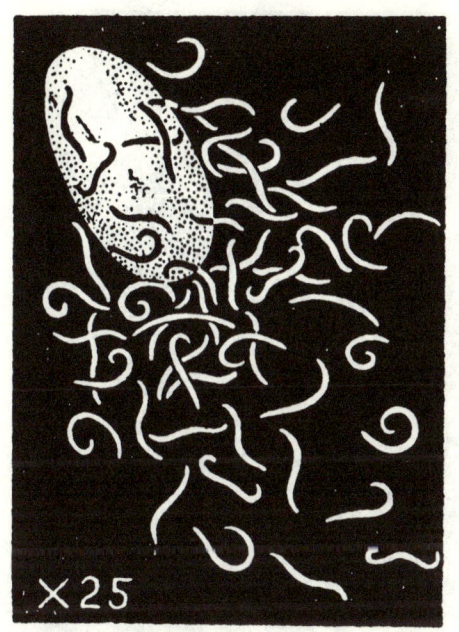

Fig. 2. Cucumber-beetle egg and the charge of nemas deposited with it.

Fig. 1. Shows relative volume of beetle and parasites. The line XY shows the actual length of the beetle.

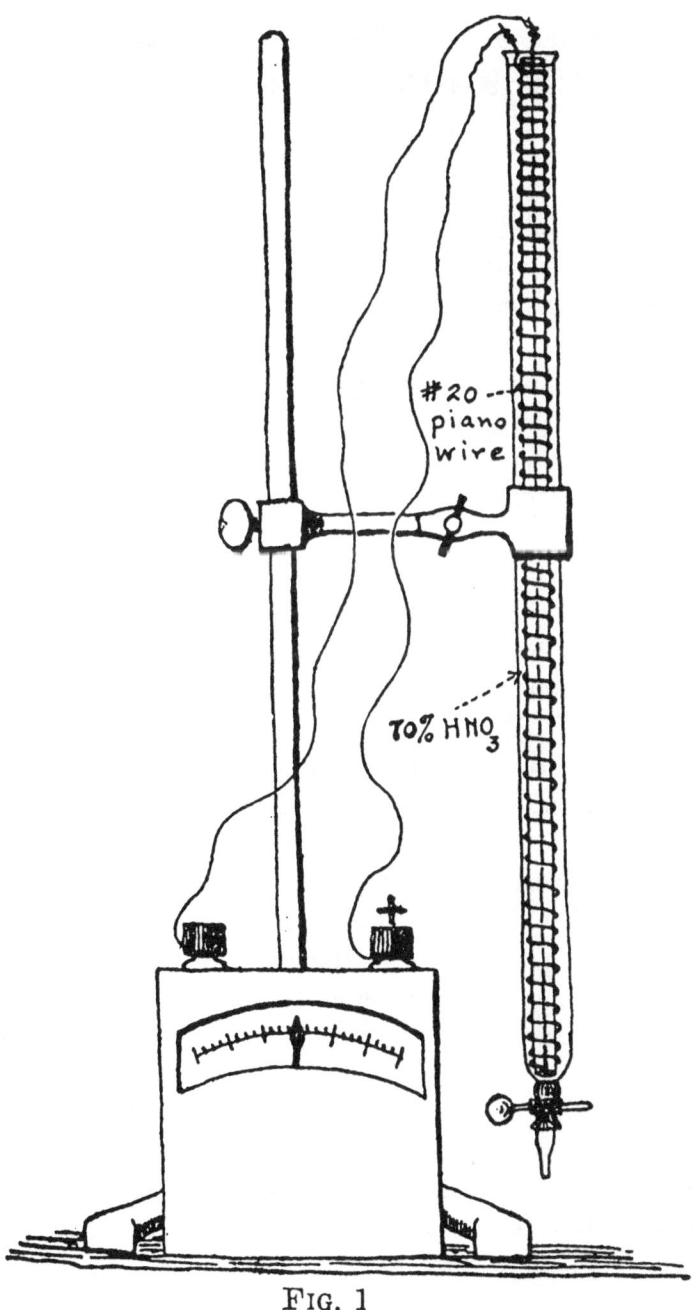

Fig. 1

Molly Tenenbaum : PREFERENCES: A PROFILE FOR PROSPECTIVE LOVERS

Parallelograms and ellipses.
Lines, as in wood grain and sediment, silk and sliced cabbage.
Salt, the crunch and shine.
Shapes moving slowly, especially gray ones.

Cats, mainly, though I'm in love with the animate snout
of Billy-the-dog, his spots
like the flecks on my earth-tone teapot.
Black pepper, lots and lots.

To walk, walk, walk, and spout opinions
of gardens: Blackberries, yes, overblown, yes;
spiky, ferny, palmy, yes—to silvers, maroons, and to all
fanned and toothed jungly air.

To close the curtain at night, but not till the last
pink smudge has rubbed the hips of the vases.

Mustard seeds jumping in ginger-oil,
cascades and tumbles in music,
bow-shakes, damped slides, anything
for texture, long as nothing, but nothing
stops fluid motion—

For language, hand, wood, stone.
Handmade, and that includes dessert.
Sawblades, wine-words, beaded purses.
Rusted tools no one remembers.

Cross-sections, captions, frontispieces.
Charts of the phrenologic head.
Cow-maps showing cuts of meat.
Coffee pots like science experiments, water in the bottom,
coffee in the middle, steam through a tube to the top.

To eat while it's hot.

To not wait. To imagine a boat
sliding the finger-troughs and knuckle-waves.

Earlobe and flat plate of sternum.
Ribs, and the heart's Chinese lantern.
Lemon, coriander, clove.

Garlic, and all the bitter greens.
Something to bear down on, something to tender,
something to hold on the tongue, stones
with feldspar windings, stones that look blue underwater,
brick-red and all the timbres of brown.

And if you've cared to read this far, I should tell you
a felt companion has walked by me always,
opens a gold space wherever I go,
has sung to me since the day I was born—
blue, sometimes, at the edges,
flaring or cooling by whatever
bellows or weather—

I don't understand it either.
I could stare forever at sky needling pine and flapping in maple.

Maybe you're sanding a mahogany table
or looking up in the book that rust-headed bird,
the one fussing up a circus of pollen in the mahonia.
I see you as through handblown glass, or not at all,

but let's eat hot pie
and listen to rain on tin.

I love the fall from a struck string like fire on a rope
and the thumbprint pool of shade at the base of a throat.
That beat, that gulp.

Molly Tenenbaum : SOLUTIONS TO THE CHECKLIST PROBLEM

Keep the check marks on separate,
    uncorrelatable pages.
Make up tasks—"brush black streak
    in throat of iris,"
    "bake individual lemon tarts,"
    and check them, regardless.
Slide the stars, unapplied, side to side
    in the dark of their box.
For every check, a chew of dirt.

For every check, a swish to spit it out.
As the teacher said of exclamation points,
    "Once a year, like birthdays."
The claw the cat flexes into the tree's stringy bark,
    the earring's glinty gold post—
    let the check-mark be anything, anything else.
So you can't tick when the urge strikes,
    clear the house of pencils completely.

Cut up appliance instruction booklets
    and paste the pieces backward.
    Let the displays flash noon.
Set the alarm for that dusty pearl time
    that could be either twilight or dawn.
Some use kava, but it leads to trouble in the kidney.
Some swear by melatonin, but it makes me dizzy.

Substitute a map of U-pick farms.
Substitute breakfast #1, two eggs and toast.
Trade with a friend: her bank, her bills,

    her groceries, her rice milk
    you don't even like. Her appointment,
    her results, her news.
Substitute your favorite palindromes.

Try it without penetration—
    it's hot.
Ask for a history first.
Use protection, and don't
    let the wet get on you.
Always pee immediately after.

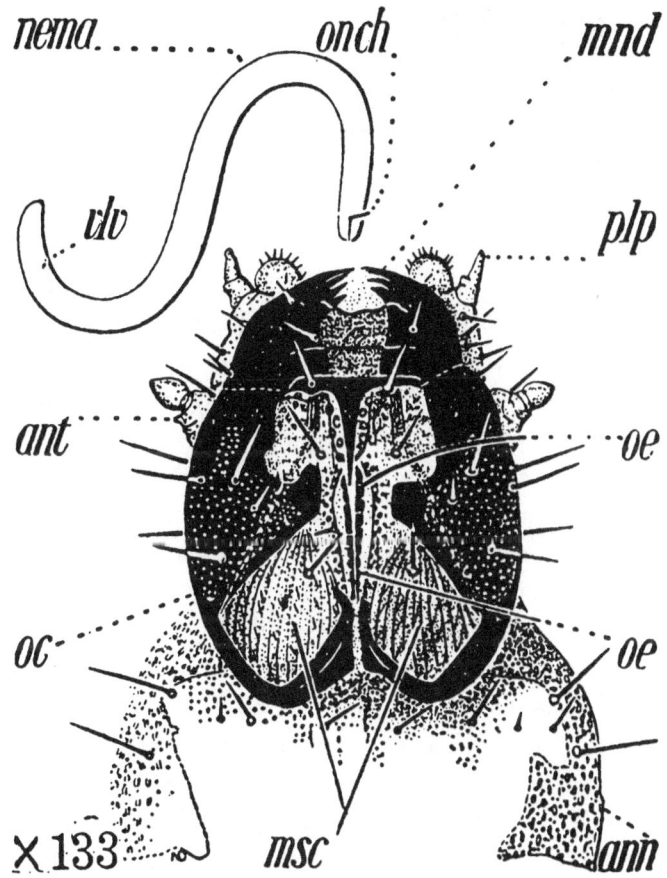

Fig. 4. Head of very young cucumber-beetle larva and of young *Howardula* at the time of its entrance. The mandibles of the grub, *mnd*, would seem to be impassable to the nema.

John Terry : WEATHER

It is a process. Now it is understood, called geophysics, tectonics, volcanism, and creep. There are still cultures who have no use for words like these, and they simply refer to it as sacred.

I could explain how Angel Falls shifts its knickpoint and is always undercutting in its efforts. The way the falls whet away weaker shale and sandstone, anchoring discharge, then spill into the braided prairie river with a borrowed name—Niobrara.

But I'm not called upon to expound today. There are no curious tourists who don't want to get too close to the thing itself, but want enough to know how it's defined by the experts with answers in that field.

It is Chris and I, consequences following actions, and it is rather simple to us as we lie bare-backed against the damp, porous stone. To us, it is always sacred. Life begins and ends in brutality. There is no need to call it anything at all.

My younger sister spent time in a hogan on the Arizona slice of the four corners where Navajo and Hopi are clustered side by side. They are still poor, still alive after the multi-million dollar promise of the uranium mines went missile and malnutrition. A small portion of our tax money, she says, keeps them drunk and educated about the fiscal potential of all their reservations. My sister split scrub mesquite so the old woman who lived in a mesa shadow could spend more time fattening goats and sheep and trying to coax the soil into produce.

Those mesas are the result of one-million years of wind shear pushing grains of sand across the floor. The mesas are cut by blowing sandy teeth, and only strength of composition lets them rise above the rest of the landscape. Scarce rain, when it falls hard, makes talus slopes in the open veins at the mesa bases.

My sister told this to the Dineh children in the schoolhouse, that they might know the curriculum. She explained this to the old widow woman, who still off-handedly calls her shadow-giving mesa sacred from the corner of her tired eyes. The children aren't too sure about what it is they're being told to call these things. They don't really care, it seems, she says, because they don't have any listeners left, and their limbs are all misshapen. They are birth defects from the dust their fathers ate in the mines.

Drizzle turns to rain, and Chris and I upturn the canoe on a dry shelf, in protest against the May Nebraska sky. We are wet enough, and the river is already swift and crafty. Still, it is safer than the highway, though our tax-dollars preserve the pavement nicely and keep it, for the most part, predictable. On the highway, at least we can see where some of the money goes.

Chris opens a beer. I light a cigarette. Rain, steadier now, bangs the canoe over our heads and runs off in a sluice before tangling itself up in river. We'll hold out, I think, until the storm blows over.

I was watching the radar, and hook echoes were red-inching towards us, said the Doppler. I got in the car drunk, and hauled in John to go chase.

There was a black stripe across the siren blaring sky, and we drove away from the town through sheeting rain, heading for the heartbeat of the bad energy.

We stopped for more beer at a Quickie outside Clinton Lake. A woman was pacing frantic nervous behind the counter. I went inside.

"Y'all see anything?"

"No ma'am, but we aim to."

All her strength was in her trembles as she made change and pressed dimes into my palms. I didn't want pity, but it came.

"Look," I said above the sirens, "see that oak out there?"

She nodded frantically, pressed a hand to her breast.

"That thing gets to bucking funny, and you get into that walk-in cooler, you hear me?"

She nodded, and terror played in her eyes. I went on in spite of.

"That thing's vacuum sealed reinforced steel, and even if this roof goes sky-high ass over teakettle, you'll be snug in there."

She started to cry. Sirens swung away and back around again. Rain thickened, and John leaned on the horn. I could feel her begging us to stay until things blew over, but her mouth couldn't follow suit, and the world ain't made easier by others protecting you from the worst of it. I snatched up the beer case and wagged my finger.

"Watch that tree like I said!" I yelled above the wind. "And don't lock this door neither! Other folks might need a safe place to be!"

John's face was sweating nervous. I handed him a beer. Pebbles scraped across the parking lot, birds flew crazy in the sky, and we headed for Osage county with hail drumming off our thin tin shield, trying to break into us both.

*

The river is creeping onto our shelf, and Chris is crying. So am I. It's not easy here, and the rain is showing no signs of letting up.

I'm thinking things through. My cousin Robert is in Iraq, shooting people up for gasoline and the stock market. He sent me a letter last month, wondering how I was doing, sad that he'd served his tour and then got another six-ten months tacked on in exchange. "It isn't easy taking someone's life," he said "especially someone you don't know. I just keep myself going by thinking about all those innocent folks dying in those twin-towers in New York, and catfishing in our favorite hole down on the `Cygnes when I come back. Wishing you well, trying not to get my ass shot off. Sincerely, Robert." I miss my cousin. I know his eyes will never be the same, over there, protecting us innocents, wading through oil-fields and the spilled brains of dead futures.

The power-lines are jumping, and John and I bump fists going after another beer. It's taking the edge off, and we need that right now. We're caught in straight-line gusts, and even full gas is veering us left as the funnel forms. Cows scream in open pastures at the horror of the present sky or the factories in their future. The man on the radio interrupts Tim McGraw's singing about where the green grass grows, watching his corn pop up in rows, and implores east Osage and west Douglas to head for basements or sturdy tubs. He says it's a big one, a mile wide, and Pomona has just been leveled.

The sign on Douglas County 1060 says Pomona, 20. The dust is sucking away towards the wind, and as we crest a bluff in Quenemo, the black source is before us, blistering the floodplain of Hundred Mile Creek and the oxbow elbows of the Marais de Cygnes. Like the sound coming through an angry fiddle when charged hand-dives force the bow, the storm grows before our eyes. The reception is lost. Even trusted airwaves have slackened and squelched into meaningless noise. All things move when prompted. All things yield to fury.

John lived through Andover and the floods of '93, same as me, and we've never seen the likes. The drunk wears off quick, death spins lumber and livestock, chewed up dreams puked out in mid-air. Somewhere in that belly is Pomona and Melvern, a general store and a post-office and a paper route, and the hunger still grows. A trooper flies by us, sirens on, a senseless blur wrapped up in a fear for life that refuses to see us sitting still on the hill-top, frozen, white, and reckoning. People afraid of their lives will tell you that all hicks are dumb, and only trash lives in a trailer. They have a sadistic urge to give everything they can't understand some kind of name.

*

Thunder mixes with the rain, and the river is coming up fast. Soaked and cold, we push the canoe up nettles, hogthistle, and coneflower, and head for the bunchgrass. We were too drunk this morning to consider dry wood, and we didn't care about the forecast. Sometimes you learn more without the sun, and life needs it all to make any kind of sense.

Chris starts singing to kill the noise and fear, and I find myself humming along. We can't stay away much longer. Folks were creased-brow wondering before we left, and spawned discussions are likely replacements by now.

It was too late. We were too awestruck and terrified to move. The car was bucking, and we knew it wouldn't hold if we didn't turn around. The rain stopped, the noise lifted, and pieces of torn apart things fell through the silence.

"Let's get the fuck out of here! We're gonna die!"

Gonna die anyway.

I peeled around on the quivering blacktop and laid into the accelerator. The rear-view held the fattening twister and ninety is faster than sixty, but the slight distance we were creating was not a safe one, or so the lurching car told us as we slid through familiar curves, praying the tires would hold.

Good things.

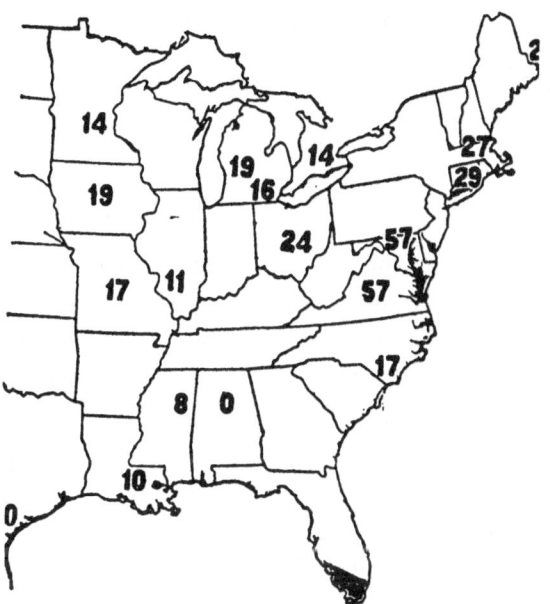

FIG. 3. The map-figures give the percentage of beetles found infested by *Howardula*. The figures for different localities a few miles apart in any given region usually were in substantial agreement. Where the percentage of infestation was highest, the nematism was highest, and vice versa. The presence of the nema does not exclude other internal parasites, such as other insects and gregarines. About 1,500 *D. vittata* were examined. Below are addresses of those who kindly contributed insects for examination.

Balduf, W. V., Marietta, O.
Cobb, Dr. F., Ann Arbor, Mich.
Cobb, V., Whitman, Mass.
Chapin, E. A., Falls Church, Va.
Fenton, E. A., Ames, Iowa.
Flint, W. P., Urbana, Ill.
Gentner, L., Lansing, Mich.
Hall, Dr. M. C., Chevy Chase, Md.
Harned, R. W., Agr. College, Miss.
Haseman, L., Columbia, Mo.
High, M. M., Kingsville, Tex.
Kelsall, A., Annapolis Royal, N. S.
Raps, E. M., Oakton, Va.
Riley, Wm. A., St. Paul, Minn.
Ross, W. A., Vineland Sta., Ont.
Smith, C. E., Baton Rouge, La.
Thomas, W. A., Chadbourn, N. C.
Walters, M. J., New London, Ct.
Watson, J. R., Birmingham, Ala.

Jen Tynes : EXCERPTS FROM *WHAT IS FOUND IN NATURE (7)*

1.

Approximately one-fourth of us is ungendered until an approach. A pass. Animals in captivity are typically expected to move in circles but we wanted to build something strange. Rusty algebra, a sagging part, inside he always hoped it would show its ass good. What it meant to suggest the sun rises and sets. Depending on her blush. The first atomic bomb, prepared by people, was dropped on Hiroshima seconds late. The developers were fond of their grandmothers but still the pipes. Weren't deep enough. Burned it off.

1.

We pull fat ticks from the dogs, the babies, one another's scalp. Danger shifts on the radio, my hands accept pleasure from being tied. Swimming last night until. Do not remember. What it feels like beneath my feet. In Italy buildings do not have a floor, hotels do not have a room, and airplanes do not have a row. It was over the fence and that is why we noticed when it was absent but not whether it had its faculties. Or was only a muscular contraction. Some grow back some bury their heads in the garden, as the story goes, until nightfall.

1.

We read minutes until it feels like an anniversary and then it is always paper, getting older. According to a chart on the wall, when it doubles you should extend right fingers into a steeple, left palm down, engage. A space will inhabit itself if nothing else insists. Water is more akin to a heart attack. She was fond of the access and she was shoulder-high, calling back until he was degenerated. There must be after all a father. A certain name you call and even a stranger has to hear there are two breathing patterns inside. There are methods of strangulation. Or its nearest subtitle: *strange me, strange me now.*

1.

Last in the row is a magnified eye that bobs on a blank stalk, breaking a lash of girls. Sometimes there is no choice, the rest of your life vibrating out of some hole. Imposed upon, a tangle. Of repetition and intent. It is divisive even to know how division works, what names. The paralympics games consisted of sports: archery, athletics, basketball, boccia, cycling, equestrian, fencing, football, goalball, judo, lawn bowls, powerlifting, shooting, swimming, table tennis, tennis, volleyball. The strongest muscle is a sentimental. Open but for those stark.

1.

A code moves between places and then place is set. It took less than a year away from each other for a father to stop recognizing a mother. In her face. The way a weight is dropped. There are towns in the world with more telephone numbers than inhabitants. They rock at each end and finally in the center. Scrap candles all balled up. Frozen u-pipes. The necks of plastic jugs.

1.

If the smalls of our backs were both painted gold we would become identical. Unable to respirate, or also breathless. A marathon runner who paced our field dropped a foot every season until it rained. Until it rained, he washed the cows' broad hides in slow circles. A finger in the roan. Girls possess (on average) square feet of skin. Unlike bolts in the back, of everything against them light moves through.

1.

The places we have scars from aren't telling what they made. Fourty-two city blocks with a burden, all morning I bled new sweaters in the sink. Foreign white terrain. Trash that presupposes boxsprings. We just need a place to settle in. It took a woman years to realize that her husband was actually a woman who used "an artificial penis." The fact of the translation is in the feet that connect to, the port that divorces, my big guns. I wonder were they careful, did it fill up the whole house.

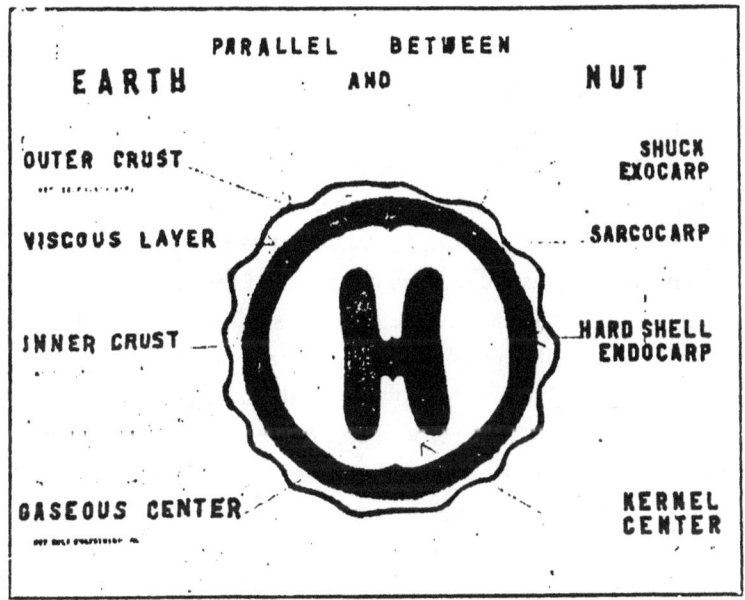

Fig. 1.

Jane Unrue : A NEW POSITION FOR THE LOWER LIP

It was winter. Wasn't it. Looked cold. Lie back. Eyes closed. Keep thinking about that picture. Winter cabin in the woods. Take good long sweeping looks across. That is. Remember everything that you were given. Windows. Empty. Sky was crisp. Reflect. Or should I say. I'll even pull the drapes so there's no need to. Snow had fallen but it seemed as if there might be something worrisome about to. Walkway peeking out from underneath the snow. Trees. Sky. And even though it's just an image in our minds let's situate ourselves within it someplace where we more effectively can watch. There's something sad you say about the walkway? Possibly the walkway I guess. Little bit. So let's all hide out in the woods not close but close enough so we can. That's right. Brad. We're focused on it. In it. Only now this image has begun to move. Smoke rises from the chimney and the windows have begun to flicker. Chrissy. In one window you can see. Look left. A figure of a man whose back is turning. In the other you can. Brad. Look right. A woman staring off into the distant reaches. Do not wave to them. Just watch them in their windows. Incidentally. You two. This room you've chosen for yourselves by picking from that copper bowl out there this is the only room that has this kind of picture on the wall above the bed. My goodness. What a lovely way to. Lucky ducks indeed. Brad. Reach your. Place your hand on Chrissy's. Lower. Brad. Eyes shut. You two. Let's fix our gazes once again. Same cabin that we just. Except there's something different now in. Brad. The window on the left is empty. Chrissy. On the right there's that same man except he hunches now as if to look at something on the floor. Not moving. Frozen there. That's right. Brad. No. They don't just disappear. Things. See. It's time you started thinking of somebody. Chrissy. Brad. Somebody other than yourselves. Don't call to them. They. In a way they're busy working. Interruption leads to. Maybe even. On the other hand you might just find that you have busted in on something truly. Think about that bowl. That numbered key. The mirror on the wall above the bed in every other room except the room that you were fortunate enough to. Close your eyes. Of course my dear I understand it tickles. Eyes closed. Good girl. Deep breath. Cabin in the woods. Where suddenly it's late. The snow has stopped. No smoke. And it is not just that our man is missing. There is something strange about the. Did you hear a latch?

Eyes closed. Look at the door. It's open. See there. Brad. A figure backs out through the. God. Whatever you do. Don't either of you make. He drags a body out onto the walkway then he turns and drags the body back. See here. Brad. I am going to tie your. Just your. Sweetie. Bear with. Inner wrists. That's right. And. Easy does it. Bedposts that's all. But while I am fooling with this stuff I'd like for you to close your eyes and both of you stay put same spot behind the trees. Breathe in. Light snow is falling. Deepest night. Our cabin seems to glow as if that fire's come back to. Eyes closed. Where you. Where they. No. The history of the picture. By the way. It's something that I think you'll come to find. In other words. This has a lot to do with how we live our lives today. They're gone of course long time ago and though the story is a rather. Doesn't really matter. All that matters is where they have ended up.

Okay. From here on out I'm going to speak as softly as. As you are finding out today it's not just watching from above and sending messages to those you've left behind by leaving pennies for example if your loved one likes to look for pennies leaving pennies in the corners of her house and in her car floor every now and. Jesus knows. It's not that kind of ending. Cabin in the woods. No more than just continuous engagement in life's awful not quite ever finished. First he clubs her. Drags her. Chrissy. Brad. Nobody's going to chop you into pieces.

All that anybody's going to. In a moment I am going whisper open up your eyes. For now. Kids. Yes. Of course he chops her into. Tries to but he can't quite get the. Deep breaths. You two. Pulling on the head until he falls asleep right in the middle of that ghastly cabin floor though when he wakes again she's in the window once again and she is staring off as if she thinks she sees the top of. What's it? Mauna Loa. He is in the other window. Turning. Slowly. Thus it all starts up again. Yes. Come to think of it. This story might be why we have a saying round these. Something that you might just find yourselves reciting to yourselves whenever you find yourselves in contemplation of the holy afterlife. Though maybe that old saying about the parking structure built on top of where their king and queen were buried hasn't got a thing to do with. Kids. Look there. Her window's empty. He is hunching over in his window as if. Mother of God. Don't call to him. You two. You can't stop this.

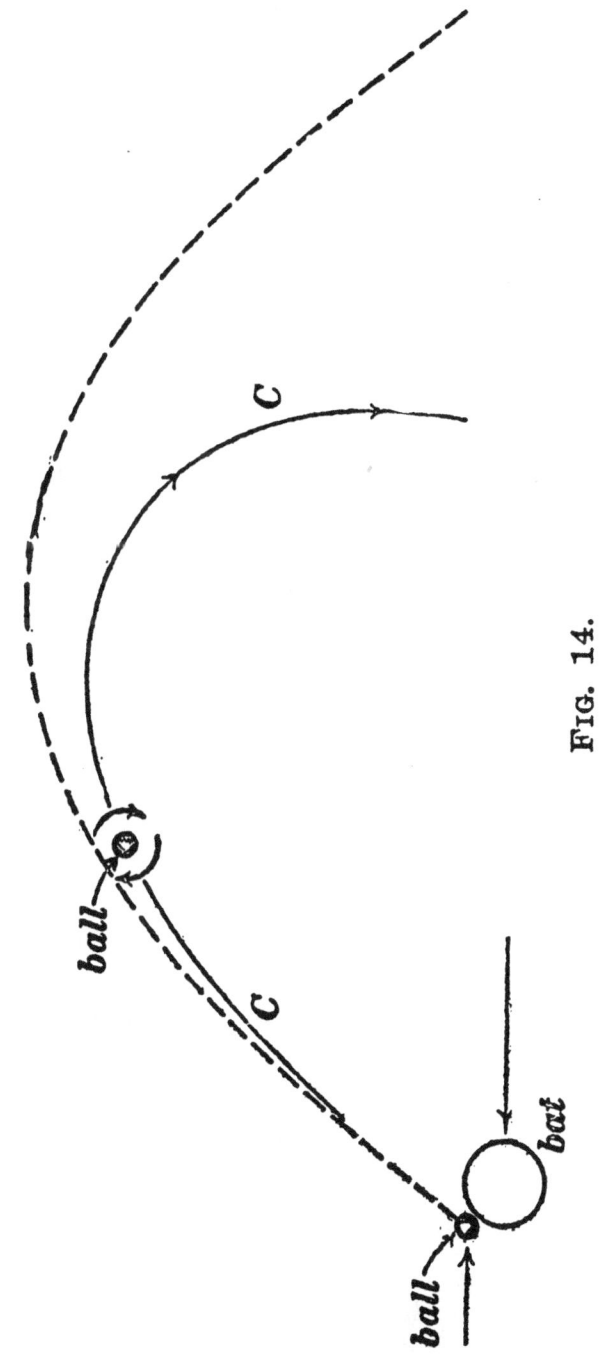

Fig. 14.

Gautam Verma : *WINTER LIGHT*[1]

        white and   shadows

    trail the lawn

                a match flare

tree shapes   flicker and flail

        clinkers in the grate

    and a gate

      yawns

          on its hinges

      [*May night more swiftly make its way* [2]

            *

somewhere in the margins a music begins

(somewhere warmth)

we cling to what's left of life in the heart's

hearth

---

[1] Title of a film by Ingmar Bergman
[2] Variant on the famous last line of Rilke's *Spanish Trilogy*

Virgil (Trans. Kimberly Johnson) : SELECTIONS FROM THE GEORGICS, BOOK 3

(lines 322-338)

But sure, when at Zephyr's summons bright summer
into clearings and pastures sends sheep and goats,
at first light of the morning star let us take to the cool
meadows, while morning's new, while grasses pale,
while dew upon the tender green most cordial to the flocks.
Then when the fourth hour of the sky has built their thirst
and with plaints the fretful cicadas shatter the woodlands,
beside wells and beside deep pools I'll bid the flocks
to drink the water rushing in oaken gutters,
in midday heat to seek a shady swale,
wherever with its ancient strength the mighty oak of Jove
spreads spacious branches, or wherever dark
with holm-oaks lush the grove lounges in holy shade.
Then offer again the trickling water and graze them again
to sunset, when cool the evening soothes the air
and the moon bedewed refreshes the thickets,
when the frith cries with the kingfisher, the furze with finch.

(394-403)

But let him whose love is for milk fetch to the stalls
lotus and clover by his own hand, and salted feed,
whence they crave streams the more, and more their udders swag,
and in their milk retain a sneaking smack of salt.
Many even keep the kids corralled from their nannies
and from the first with iron muzzles cap their mouths.
What they milk at daybreak or in daylight hours

at night they press, and what at sunset or at night they milk
at first light carry off in baskets (if to town a goatherd go),
or touch it with scant salt and lay it in for winter.

(414-439)

Learn to smudge your stalls with fragrant cedar,
with fennel smoke to rout out noisome watersnakes.
Often beneath unscoured cribs the viper lurks,
death to touch, recoiling from the sun uneasy,
or else an adder—wont to climb into the roof and from its shelter
(bitter plague of oxen) sprinkle venom on the cattle—
hugs the ground. Grab stones in hand, grab cudgels, shepherd,
and as he coils up his threats and puffs out his hissing neck,
clobber him. Now in flight, low he ducks his cowered head
while the twines of his guts and his trailing tail-tip
unwind, and the last coil drags its slow knots.
And then there's that dire serpent in Calabrian dells,
twisting her scaly back with upreared breast
and streaked with big splotches on her long belly,
who—while any streams yet jet from their fountainhead,
while the earth oozes under spring humors or stormy southwinds—
works the turlough, and holing up on shore implacable
she crams her venom-black maw with fish and chattering frogs.
Later when the marshland's parched, when the soil gapes with heat,
she dives onto dry land, and rolling her fiery glare
furies through the fields savage with thirst and panicked by the heat.
O let me not hanker to woo easy sleep
beneath an open sky nor to loll among the grasses along a timbered ridge,
when then, her molt sloughed off, fresh and sleek with youth
she winds, leaving hatchlings or eggs in her nest,
craning toward the sun, and flickering at the mouth with a three-
forked tongue.

Benjamin Vogt : FLAT TIRE

I'm chained to Chevrolets, rusted trucks,
the sound of things along the highway, pitched
revolver cries of mufflers sputtering death.
Beside the shoulder, melting into weedy dirt,
are half-blown tires, shards of glass and bolts
that angered business men and flew like gods.
Each morning I drive more slowly, right lane
the impenetrable fortress moving, seen
in instants by passing Mustangs, near-colliding
Impalas. Somewhere parts are shaking loose,
the fibrous man-made whole will give itself
to errant twists, desire poured from impulse
of arms and legs, desire to go now, that
all going must be now—that all becoming
is linked to losing bits of self by noon.

Benjamin Vogt : COMPATIBLE

Are the trees and the interstates
among them? Jet planes in erratic
white cumulonimbus? Dandelions
in cracks of city sidewalks?

And you ask day after day what
these things mean, if black is not
really white, if it can ever be,
if lack is really intense fulfillment

and we—so focused on the shallow
pool of our language—just don't
recognize this joy. If you could
touch me right now, would you?

What if your body evacuated
into mine like a levee spilled
on the town? The difference
between reclamation and possession

is inundation. And you ask
if this is good or bad and I say
irony is sublime and leads
to transcendence. And you muse

on the spider behind your shades
that won't come out, your can
of poison ready to spill upon its
body, then scream and back away

once it reveals itself leg by leg—
its shadow more mercurial than desire.

G. C. Waldrep : HEAVE-HO

if I could lift the cold from the dress form of this present *yes*
then there's a wildness we wouldn't be missing, a single revelation
spun out into series like kitchen furniture. What originates as abstraction
evolves into fluorescent pulse; in this way the transcendent
becomes useful, that is, acquires an ethical component
unlike the animals in their dull idyll.
Granted some concepts are difficult to grasp. What I can't make out
is the monogram your arrival etches in the sink's dry teething.
—But if the articulation of consent is plural?
Then we dance to supravariant tunes, self-portrait of the poet
as Deaf Man Waltzing: a terrible pun but a more elegant prospect,
not to mention less wasteful of electricity.
So let's talk blame. Last week in Ellettsville, Indiana,
I misread GUITAR LESBIANS for GUITAR LESSONS on a
    streetside sign.
They're out there, strumming away. My own risk in love
is that some continents will rise or fall before you say your first word.
We could all wear silk armbands to show who's chosen silence.
We could stand very near water and pretend to be bridges,
then others would spraypaint news of their own affections on our thighs
in bright colors. You think I'm joking. But in my dreams
someone is always cutting the bolts from my back.
Try imagining the theoretical as a succession of indigenous archetypes:
predestination, evolution, relativity :: ram, salamander, jackal.
This is the phylum of subjectivity, the genus of cohesion.
After the twenty-fourth dimension our own alphabet's exhausted;
beyond that—pictographs, ideograms, every horseshoe crab
    that scuttles
could be a proposition by Augustine or the unquiet shade
of that blender we junked last fall. Seriously,
I *demand* a ghost for each machine, I proclaim the acceptable year

of the small power tool. Where's Arthur Murray when I need him?
Wait, it's still a bright spring morning here in Pangaea.
We'll trip the heavy fantastic—watch out for my buttress, don't
    scuff the linoleum.
You say: *He believed large fictions about himself and extended them
    onto paper.*
I say: *Infidelity*—for now, buzz of an unseen fly.

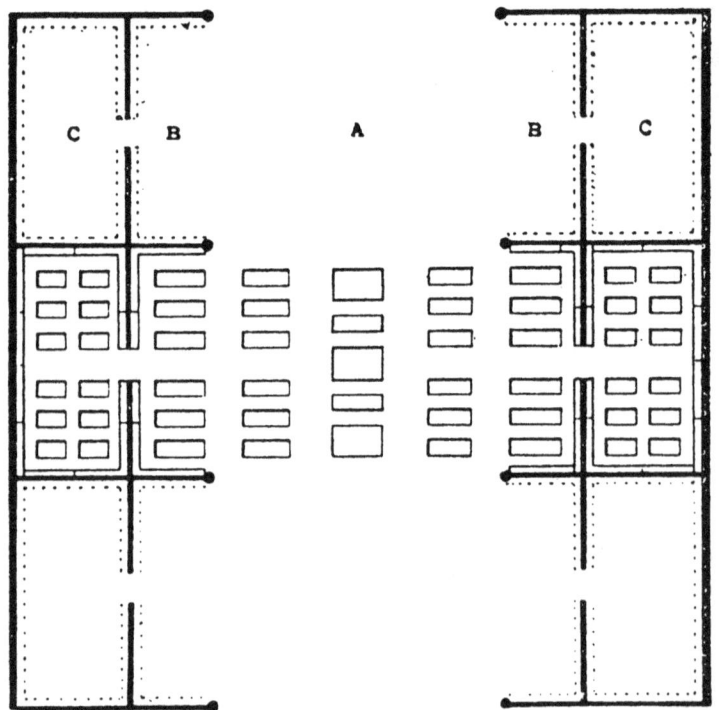

FIG. 3. Floor plan of extensive geo-ethnic unit showing overflow into lateral halls, C, C. One full-sized family group and two auxiliary lay-figure groups are provided for besides a large number of associated and auxiliary exhibits.

Fritz Ward : DEAR

At the end of love there is a stove.

At the end of suffering a snowman naked down to the charcoal briquettes.

At the end of earth a shower drain tangled with black hair.

At the end of day an electric fence crackling in the rain.

At the end of night a runway from which all dreams depart.

At the end of death clarified butter.

At the end of sky a space. At the end of space a wishing well.

At the end of all beginnings a door like any other, dividing inside from out.

Fritz Ward : LETTER TO MY ARSONIST

I can't put a finger on the first spark,
can't say where the smoke started, or when.
But it started. It mattered. It changed
matter.

If asked, I'd say you're closer to my nightmares
than to my parents, or that you're a child
of every war I've ever fought
with myself. That's okay,

even the sky has a second story
to tell, and it's not always heaven.

Sometimes, it's your father looking down
at the fresh story of blood across your chin,
a soon-to-be scar written with your awkward
adolescence and the driveway gravel—He answers,
You're a man,
        and this means almost nothing:
                      cock and chromosomes,
                      balls and breath. Almost
nothing.

But-Oh-Maybe,
if your mother had touched
        the ruined door of your face—

But-Oh-Maybe-Not.
God might still be the first curtain
of flames, the book of matches
still a hymnal in your pocket,

      and the night—
But what does it matter?

      The night *is*
a basement of broken furniture
and the cracked-glass faces of relatives
face down in the dust, or, for the lucky few,
stacked face to face, their lips inches from touching.

The nights you find yourself delivered
to an empty house on a country road,
there's no denying the brief triumph of fire.
      The smolder and glow. The argument
of oxygen and ash.

You kneel and stare down through the basement
window, where just now it's beginning
to take shape: a room of orphaned light
and kindling, where the scripture of flames
is just another metaphor for emptiness—
      and the faces, brightly lit, refuse the rain.

Fritz Ward : MEMO ON THE EVOLUTION OF PARKING GARAGES

Let's be honest: the sun's incessant sermon
of starlight is too much. The three grains of rock salt
dissolving on the ice-covered street reveal nothing
about devotion. Often enough, love is weaker

than gravity. Now let's be dishonest:
here, I'll offer you this vision of a cardinal
stationed in the pin oak, a red ransom note
illuminating the window, desire incognito.

Feathered red and sprinkled with lice,
the metaphor is marked for illness, for a hospital window
painted shut in Syracuse. Here, let's watch the patient
as she watches a nest of crooked twigs and gray string slowly

untangle. Now it's your turn: I want an alley
of snow and cigarette butts beyond the oak tree.
A man with six coats pissing his initials
into the hour-old snow. He'll answer my uncertainty

by explaining the evolution of parking garages:
how the exhaust gathering in the corners translates into a warmth
that lingers till midnight. To be honest, the man is a flower-
potted drunk. He adorns the alley. The leaves of his hands unfold

for loose change. But he's not even mine, not unless
—No, not even then. You can take him from me, if,
for a moment, you believe there's one person
you were meant to save. If you describe the trembling

hands, the dried blood decorating his zipper. Only if
he'll save you with his need. Only if you remember
you're my mother and not dementia's angel. But maybe
I want to keep this season of self-deception: leaves resurrecting

the hills, a red metaphor on a gray branch,
the therapy of acid rain seeping into the basement, flooding
the family portraits of discontent—flooding my life
with honesty, which was only ankle-deep to begin with,

barely deep enough for the drowning. But the truth
is less convincing than snow, and the truth is, I want to hurt
you. Just a little. Just enough to make you turn this page
and lie with me a little longer.

Joshua Marie Wilkinson : GIN RUMMY

If each story
     depends on the part
          the teller forgets...
Boy scatter. Sleeping pill
            sleep & the twisted
out splinter in my arm from the dream.

In the movie
the man tears out the page in the phone book

at the pancake house. These aren't even movie sets.
This really is Arkansas. Black-fisted, tire swing,
bird shatter. The kiss dried on your face.

One woman kicks another in the bathroom stall,
the dog returns through the cracks in the fence,

Another question which starts with the word if
just brings a man to the ground slowly
like ellipses & a paragraph break.

Swimming in the river
where the cattle trundle around.

A snake in the dead boy's mouth.
The wife of the churchyard
caretaker who bleaches her face in the bathroom.

Gin rummy. Your slick way of saying alright
like granddad.

I've come all the way back
by three busses, night fog & a little whatchyacallit
to the funeral. Somebody

mistakes your uncle
for your father
                                    at the reception.
  It occurs to me that even music
                            wouldn't do this to us
      without first
      asking for a dance.

Susan Settlemyre Williams : ALBUQUERQUE, YOUR ASHES IN MIDAIR

Your brown empty city. The desert's out
of flower. Nothing holds it, grain

on grain. Light as sky in my palm,
in a blue ice cream carton, I hold the gray

soft feathers of your ash. Which will be set
in the brass pan against the other brass pan

that holds the feather of truth. Weighing,
nothing on nothing—I'm wrong, it's the heart

that's weighed. Your dust doesn't balance
anything; it hangs a long time in the heat,

lifts on an updraft. In storm season once
I flew through desert thunderheads rising

in giant chimneys, miles above
the plane. I don't understand weightlessness

or perfect balance, the boy hired to take out
my half-uprooted, leaning pine, how

he roped himself to it, walked upright its tilting
height. Left-handed, he chain-sawed

a branch on the left, then right-handed, one
on the other side, stood on their stumps and slashed

limbs, one hand and one hand, and balanced
on *those* stumps, and the dust

didn't fall at all, it seemed, sand-colored,
only hover and lift, until I couldn't watch him

step onto sky, how he swung himself
out on his rope and glided to earth, in three

strokes brought down the armless trunk.
The sky had no clouds, and the limbs

were slow and brown, but the ground shuddered
each time one came down on the tattered

chrysanthemums. The boy hung in the air
like his weight was nothing up there.

I don't understand how the body can be burnt
into nothing, this little plume I let go.

When I dreamed of Suzanne come back,
she had no more weight than you, but she glowed

and her milk-blind eyes had turned
to aquamarines. I want you radiant like her,

not dust hovering in brown summer air.

Susan Settlemyre Williams : LOST

Sweet bite of loam.
She remembers that and sky peeling open.
Her wrist gashed with lily-pollen,
then the long hot where grass casts a net
over her face. Nothing more? Not the ragged
sneaker flown where someone beating
a pattern of seeking into the field will miss it.
Not the rustle, blow from behind, furtive
blade of pain. Not the pulling down, great weight
of breath slithering out of her body. Random,
what remains and what is a scatter
of glass. How none of it matters here
in the rhythmless dark in which she's sinking,
cold dark where nothing will ever move,
where seeker and pattern are only
their own distant call and answer
and then broken like stones.

Susan Settlemyre Williams : SILHOUETTE

Defined by what's cut away:
Last name. Breast.
What's left after the cutting is silence.

White bath. Snow light on gray walls.
Two rooms close and cold as a snow fort.
The windows look blank

on other walls, a flat roof. I tilt the blinds
till nothing comes in but light. In the stillness
the razor's snick on my legs is loud.

And why bother? No one will know how
smooth I am all over. Ice sculpture
under the surgeon's white scrawl.

All the color cut away. I forget
if I have color sealed inside. I only see
how sleek my vacancy has grown.

Once I went out at two a.m.
to watch the meteors. I lay down on the pavement
and disappeared. Over me, stars

blindly scribbled the dark, their flight
sudden, then broken off.

Steven Wingate : CAESURAE

There are many beautiful words
wedged between what we discarded
and what we have lost. Words bringing knowledge
to the unsophisticated so they may be
    as lost
        in sophistry
            as we.

There are many beautiful words in this poem
including harmony
    transmogrification
    conifer
    undulating
    crosstabulation
    misanthropy
    and bittersweet
but its original intention
is to deceive you into believing that words
are not beautiful. That the human mind
is not capable of sustaining the wonder
that lies on the tongue when such words
pass by and bless it.

There are many beautiful words in this poem
including scintillating
    Magyar
    bouffant
    antediluvian
    furlong
    diphthong
    and thistle

but its original intention
is to make you remember the odors you favored
as a child. The smell of fresh lemon peel
or of sweetly-scented birthday candles.
Of the prized uncle's cigar
or the apples that fell ripe
    from the tree
        into your hand.

There are many beautiful words in this poem
including tapestry
    divination
    insectivore
    cuspidor
    protoplasm
    bicuspid
    and molar
but its original intention
is to cause you consternation (another
beautiful word) as you think of the blank spaces
between them. Of your mouth's emptiness
as another word rises and waits to fly from it

dreaming that you will send it to a distant mountain
to shimmer in quick harmony
with the wind in the snow-frosted trees.

Mark Yakich : B-SIDE: "THE MOUNTAIN"

This poem begins with a line found under my sister's hat as it laid on a bench in the European wing of the Metropolitan Museum of Art. We weren't even looking at the Balthus painting "The Mountain" from which the poem derives its innovative name. The poem was first called "Seven Ways of Dying a Little Girl's Hair," but I couldn't decide on a color. The knife-sharpening of the pencil halfway through the poem actually happened. Every morning our father would take a kitchen knife and sharpen our pencils. He made it look so easy that one morning I decided I would try. That is how I lost a good chunk of flesh from the knuckle of my left index finger. It didn't hurt until I saw the blood. That's when I fainted. When I came to, my sister was fanning me with one of our grandfather's dirty handkerchiefs. Our grandfather lived with us until I was 12. He lived in the den because he had no legs with which to climb the stairs; they had been shot off in so-called Big One. The walls of the den were lined with books, so that every time I went in to see him I felt as if he were the smartest man on earth. The books, my mother's and father's, were all nonfiction.

Mark Yakich : B-Side: "THE ORDINARY SUN"

New Yorkers assume that the pastoral scene depicted here takes place in Central Park. Chicagoans assume the location is Grant Park. Parisians believe it to be Jardin du Luxembourg. Of course this is only pointed out because one should appreciate the power of people's intuition. Nevertheless, the poem takes place in Gori, Georgia, in 1889. The boy in the poem, who has stolen his father's razor, is J.V. Stalin. And the "unknown end" is the imminent deaths of eight million intuitions by his verbal signature. The light at the end of the poem is symbolic of the kind of life one wishes to lead but can't because one has been born a human being, a Cossack, a daughter. The absence, therefore, that surrounds the poem makes the light work hard.

Jake Adam York : ELEGY FOR JAMES KNOX

Whose 1924 death at Alabama's Flat Top Coal Mine led to the abolishment of the state's convict-labor lease system.

Because a shackle is never enough
to hold a man, but only his body,
and because the body must be made
to hold the man, to join with the chain
until the grip is overwhelming,
they took you from the prison
and sold your labor, your body
for five dollars a month, into the mine
to dig coal for Birmingham's furnaces,
the heat already pressing in on you
like a hand, the coal dust
in your lungs' own flexings
lacerating breath right out of you
little at a time, the hard pump of the arms
speeding it up in the candle-lit dark
that lay on your skin the way
they already saw you, a density
to be burned so iron could rain
from rock, purified and bright.
But to take you out, the hands
sudden from the tight, dark heat,
and beat you with a wire
spun from the kind of steel
you had begun to forge in the shaft,
to return your muscles' work this way
till you were red as ore, and then
to tie and dip you in a laundry vat
and boil the hair from your body

as if it were any pig, and then
call it suicide, as if you had done this
to yourself, to say you drank
bichloride of mercury instead of sweat,
instead of blood, instead of heat
and coal and *nigger*, to rule it
poison, to inject your dead body
with corrosive metal and call it
another day at the office, ready
to do it all again should the sun rise,
God willing, to ship the coal out
to charge the ironworks so someone else
could draw you from the hearth
for forging a thirty dollar check
in Mobile, and burn you into textbooks,
something dark to be turned
like this chip of iron I finger
as I think of you,
a small, hard strip of Alabama
that's losing, that's turning back
red as the clay that buries it all—
was it ever, will it ever be, enough?

Scott Zieher : GRAND AIR AND DUST

And thus the four walls of home were done
Just so, with no windows and no door yet
And this, like a blank page, became them

Then they cut the jambs through a thick wall
With a hammer they made their eastern way
Together. Their flickering afforded floatlight

To all four corners. A very big hole they carved
In the middle of the western wall. A window
To the north was what they needed next.

And so the hammer was heavy for their small idea
And thus they took to fists and a good, strong awl.
It was Chalk Sunday but they were in Mexico.

And blessed by the opposites of wall and hole, fence
And gate, door and way, they proceeded to and fro
By dint of understanding their simple domestic limit.

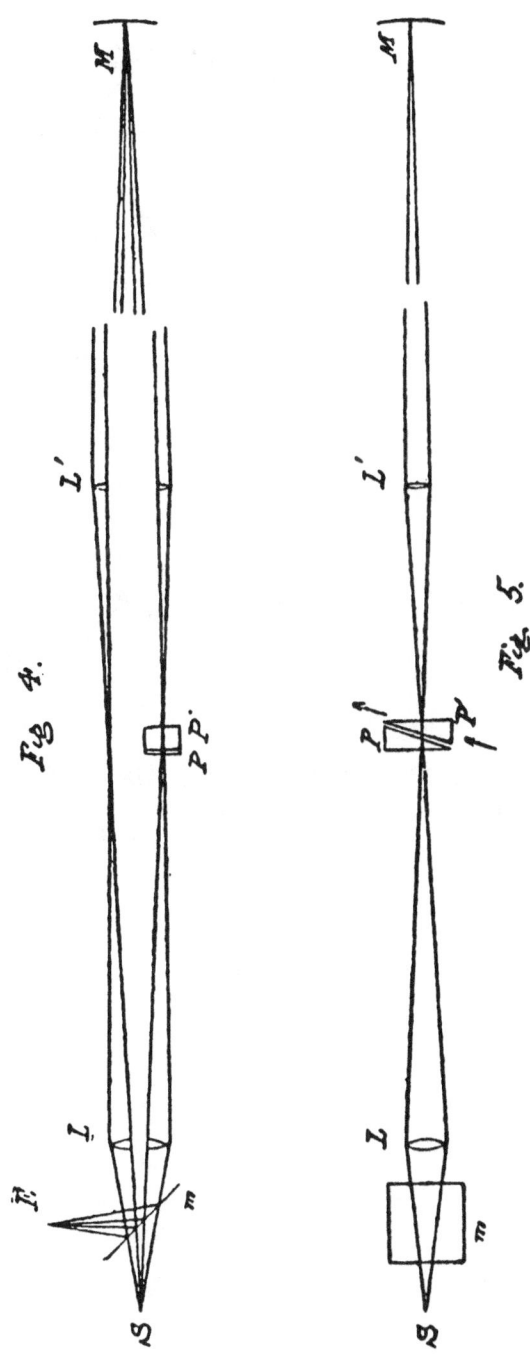

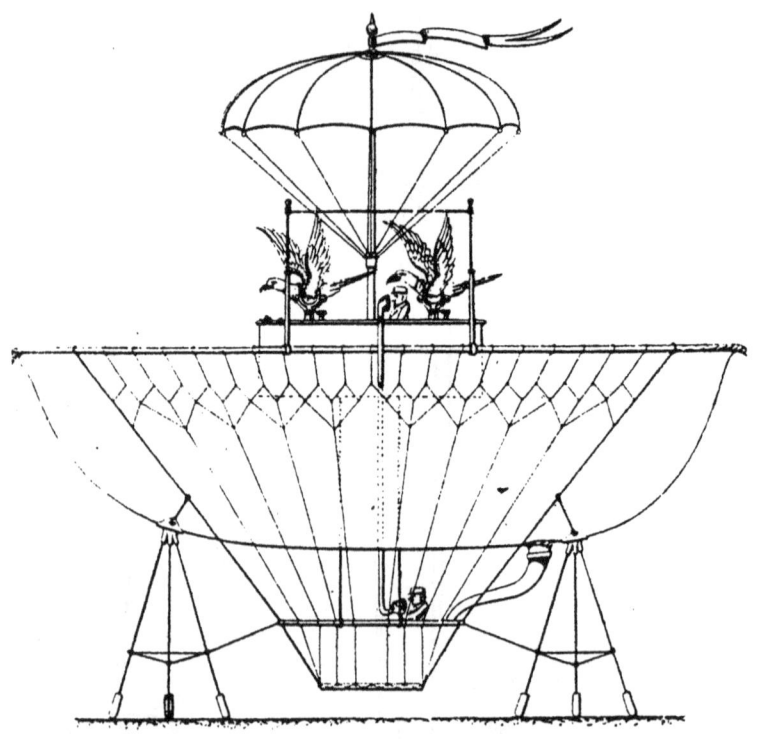

The Forerunner of the Flying Machine.
A peculiar apparatus patented by a Frenchman for propelling and guiding balloons.

Acknowledgments

We have opted to omit contributor bios in this print anthology, as they're all available online with the magazine proper (you know the address by now, right?), and on account of who cares? Let the work speak for itself. Then go Googling if you like. It'll be, like, awesome.

THE IMAGES HEREIN, unless noted otherwise, originally appeared in issues of *Science* magazine published between 1902 and 1921.

THE IMAGES ON PAGES 144 AND 145 were published in *Forrester's Playmate*, issue Jan.-June 1856.

IMAGES ON PAGES 59, 100, AND 254 originally appeared in an issue of *Leslie's Weekly* from 1899.

IMAGES ON PAGES 8, 14-15, 20, 40, 44-45, 108, 158, 221, AND 225 originally appeared in *The Scientific Monthly* from 1902 to 1911.

"Spring Styles in Hats" on page 27, "Rebuilding a Brain" on page 33, and "'Success Chart of Spring and Summer Collars" on page 70 originally appeared in *Success Magazine*, March 1906. "Race Chart" on page 155 originally appeared in an ad for *Ridpath's History of the World* that appeared in *Success Magazine*, March 1907. Thanks to the Campbell family for these.

And one big thanks to all of our contributors, readers, and supporters. We would not exist without you.

And for the type geeks, the text here is set in Jenson, with titles in Futura.

www.ingramcontent.com/pod-product-compliance
Lightning Source LLC
Chambersburg PA
CBHW051750040426
42446CB00007B/300